Marx's Capital Illustrated

Marx's Capital Illustrated

Das Kapital

David Smith

Illustrated by
Phil Evans

Updated Edition

Haymarket Books   Chicago, Illinois

I dedicate my share of this book to Laura, with love.
Many thanks to my wonderful family—Robin, Daniel,
Laurie, Violet, and Elliott—for a lifetime of inspiration.
—David Smith

- and my share of this book is for Polly.
Phil Evans

Original text © 1982, David Smith
Epilogue © 2014, David Smith

Illustrations © 1982, Phil Evans
New art © 2014, Daniel Smith (pages 36, 69, 176, 185, 195, 200, 207)

First published by Writers and Readers Publishing Cooperative, London.
This edition published in 2014 by Haymarket Books
PO Box 180165
Chicago, IL 60618
773-583-7884
info@haymarketbooks.org
www.haymarketbooks.org

Trade distribution:
In the US, Consortium Book Sales and Distribution, www.cbsd.com
In Canada, Publishers Group Canada, www.pgcbooks.ca
In the UK, Turnaround Publisher Services, www.turnaround-uk.com
In Australia, Palgrave Macmillan, www.palgravemacmillan.com.au
All other countries, Publishers Group Worldwide, www.pgw.com

ISBN: 978-1-60846-266-7

Cover image by Phil Evans.

Published with the generous support of Lannan Foundation
and the Wallace Global Fund.

Library of Congress Cataloging-in-Publication data is available.

Entered into digital printing March, 2021.

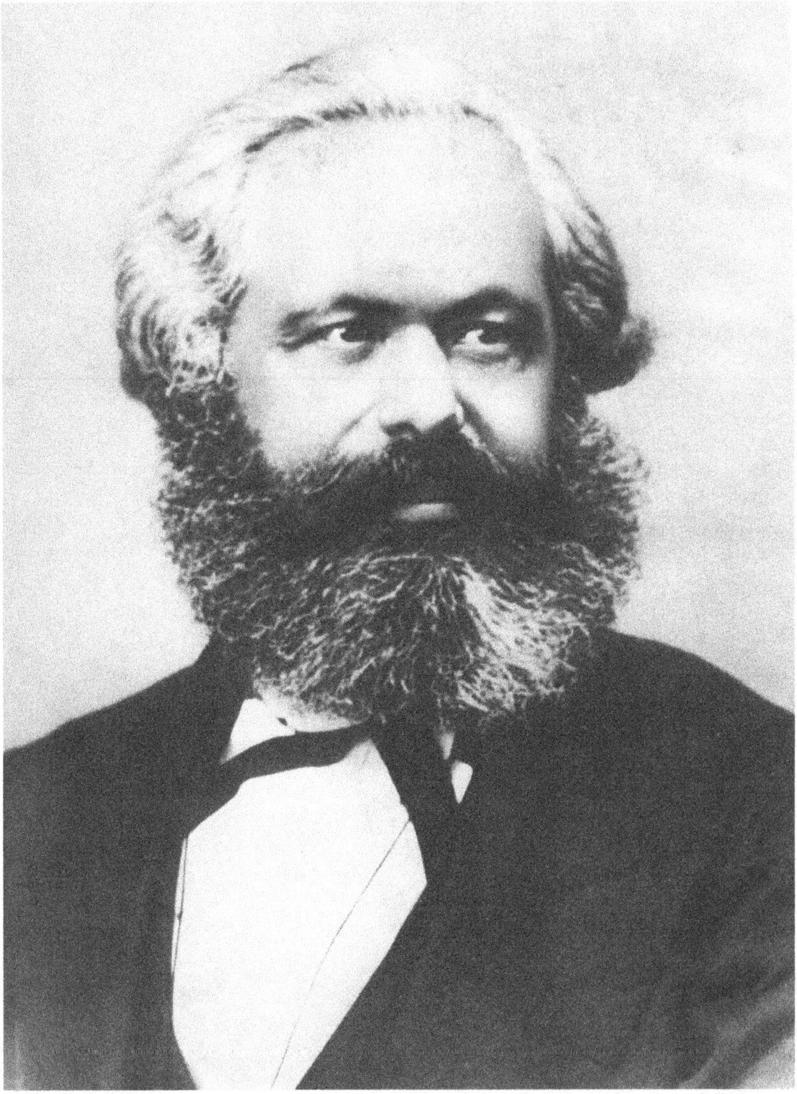

Karl Marx

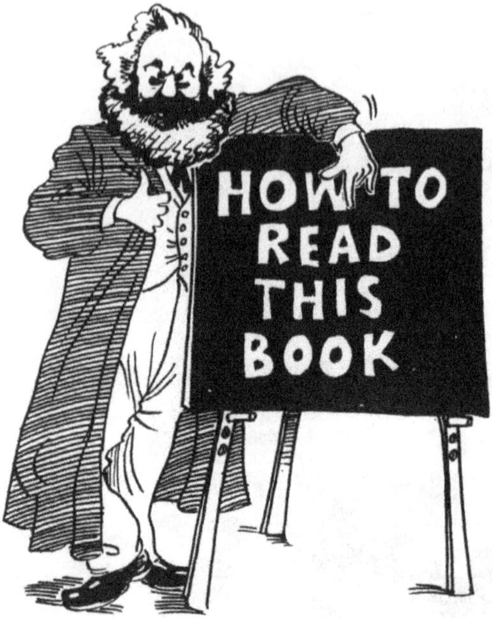
HOW TO
READ
THIS
BOOK

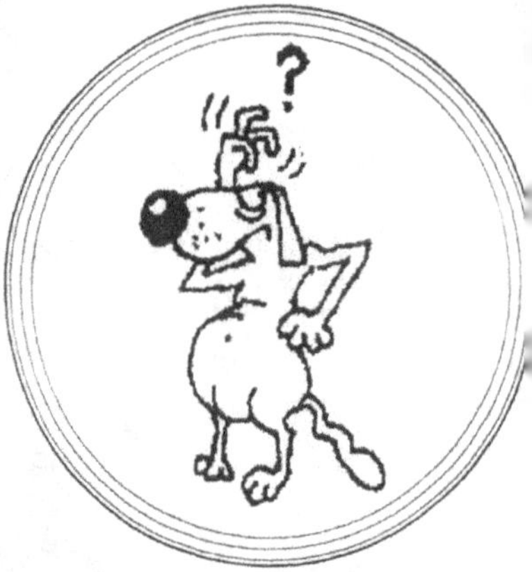
?

START HERE...

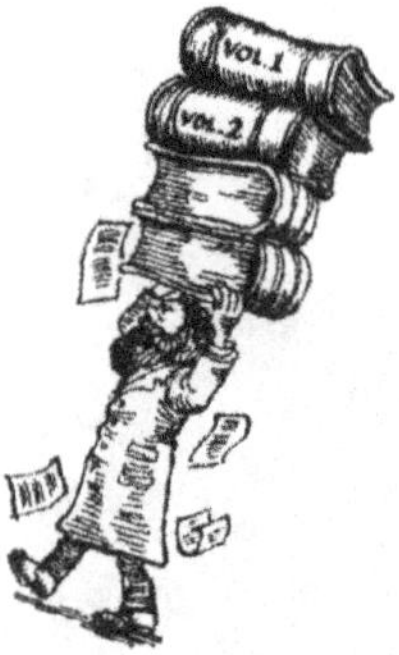
VOL.1
VOL.2

FINISH HERE...

Epilogue (2014)

The Crash and After
Capitalism in Crisis?

Karl Marx was born in Trier, Germany, near the French border, in 1818. This was just after the Napoleonic wars, one year before **David Ricardo** published his pathbreaking work, *The Principles of Political Economy*.

DAVID RICARDO 1772–1823

The industrial revolution was well underway (Watt had invented the steam engine in 1769) and factory production was sweeping Europe.

After receiving a doctorate in philosophy from the University of Jena, Marx soon turned to revolutionary politics. He arrived at the conclusion that capitalism oppresses and exploits working people. Analysing *how* this happens, and organising working people to replace capitalism with communism, became Marx's lifelong preoccupation.

Marx remained an ardent revolutionary until his death in 1883. He never wavered in his conviction that the working class can--and must--abolish production for profit, and build, instead, a society based on 'freely associated labour' engaged in production for use.

7

Neue

Rheinische Zeitung

Organ der Demokratie.

№ 301.   Köln, Samstag, den 19.   10.

Though **Capital** was Marx's life-work—a gigantic multi-volumed project started in the mid-1840's and never completely finished—Marx was hardly an armchair revolutionary.

GEORGE HEGEL   LUDWIG FEUERBACH

As editor of the *Rhenish Gazette* in 1842, in backward, absolutist Prussia, Marx (then only 24) was quickly immersed in politics. Already a radical philosopher—an exponent and critic of **Hegel** and **Feuerbach**—Marx was deeply impressed by an uprising of Silesian weavers, and by the misery and oppression of the Moselle wine-growers.

As a journalist, Marx *took sides* in the battles he reported, putting forward a radical defence of the rebel Silesian weavers and strongly arguing for their democratic rights.

The Prussian authorities grew increasingly unhappy with Marx, deciding, after several months, to suppress the *Rhenish Gazette* altogether. So dramatic was this turn of events in the eyes of Marx's German contemporaries that Marx became a celebrity of sorts—shown in one editorial cartoon as the mythical, **Prometheus,** chained to a rock in punishment for stealing the fire of the gods —to share with suffering humankind.

WORKERS OF ALL LANDS UNITE – YOU HAVE NOTHING TO LOSE BUT YOUR CHAINS !

–AND YOUR LIVER IF YOU'RE PROMETHEUS !

Marx became both a celebrity and an exile. The Prussians unceremoniously booted him out.

From this point on, Marx's odyssey begins. Expelled from Germany, Marx went to France—where he was again expelled ... to wind up, finally, in England, years later.

In France, Marx converted to socialism. The first fruits of Marx's initial foray into economics included *The Holy Family*, published in collaboration with Frederick Engels in 1843.

In 1845, Marx signed a contract for 'a book of economics'. Thinking he would finish this book quickly, Marx little realised that the project would soon grow out of hand. It would get bigger and bigger ...

Marx often had this problem. In 1851, he told Engels that

As it happened, *16 years* elapsed before even Volume one of **Capital** was published. The remainder of the work wasn't published until after Marx's death, with Engels as editor.

Soon after Marx began his intensive work on economics, Karl and Jenny were thrown out of France—as 'politically undesirable' aliens.

Moving to Brussels, Marx joined the secret League of the Just, a radical workers'organisation which soon changed its name to the *Communist League.* Engels joined, too. After completing his first published work on the capitalist economy—an essay against Proudhon entitled *The Poverty of Philosophy* (1847)— Marx was asked to collaborate with Engels on *The Manifesto of the Communist League,* better known as *The Communist Manifesto.* This incomparably famous pamphlet, encapsulating Marx and Engels' theory of the class struggle, was issued in 1848, 'the year of revolutions'.

Revolutions broke out in France, Germany, Hungary and elsewhere in 1848. They were revolutions of the rising capitalist class against feudal reaction, combined with revolts of artisans and workers. Marx and Engels rushed back to Germany to publish the *New Rhenish Gazette*.

OOH-ER! A DESPERATE BAND OF ARMED MEN!

It was in the pages of this revolutionary democratic newspaper that Marx published the series of lectures he had first delivered in 1847, *'Wage-Labour and Capital'*.

NEW RHENISH GAZETTE! CLASS WAR – LATEST RESULTS!

15

After the defeat of the revolution in Germany, Marx was tried for sedition. But after a stirring speech to the jury, he was acquitted.

Even so, Karl and Jenny were booted out of Germany again. This time, they went to England, where Engels settled, too. (His father owned a factory in Manchester.)

-AND FOR MY NEXT TRICK-

DAD OWNS THE WORKS!

WE'LL SEE ABOUT THAT!

Marx began 12 years of work as a foreign correspondent for the *New York Herald Tribune* and several other newspapers, including the *Vienna Presse*.

16

At first, Marx and Engels tried to keep the Communist League alive, but they soon decided it was no longer useful. Without a mass movement to sustain it, the group was becoming an émigré sect, splitting hairs in political isolation.

YES IT IS.

NO IT ISN'T

◎卍✻ ☆◎!

VOTE!

VOTE!

NO IT IS!

Marx devoted himself to journalism and the study of capitalism

PHOOEY! I'M OFF TO THE BRITISH MUSEUM!

SPLIT HARE

In 1858, Marx's studies had progressed to the point that he was able to draft a 1,400-page outline of his entire projected critique of political economy'. This outline, known as the *Grundrisse,* is a major work in its own right, presaging most of the themes in **Capital.** It is a *tour de force* of incomparable breadth and insight.

17

In 1859, Marx published *A Contribution to the Critique of Political Economy*, summarizing some of the basic ideas developed in the *Grundrisse*. This is an extremely valuable prologue to **Capital,** far more important for the understanding of Marx's 'theory of value' than is often realized. It is even more thorough than **Capital** on the question of money ....

In 1865, as a leading member of the *International Workingman's Association* (which had just formed and soon became a sizeable body), Marx replied at length to an argument against strikes by another key member of the group, **John Weston**, a carpenter.

DON'T COME CRYING TO US WHEN **YOU** FIND YOURSELF ON STRIKE, WESTON!

Marx's reply, later published in pamphlet form by his daughter **Eleanor,** expresses in a concise form many of his most vital ideas. These ideas won general approval in the IWA (perhaps better known as the 'First International'),

ELEANOR MARX

VALUE, PRICE, AND PROFIT

At long last, in 1867, Volume One of **Das Kapital** rolled off the presses, to be greeted immediately and warmly in the workers' press. The capitalist press ignored it entirel

Marx felt that he had reached an important milestone with the publication of **Das Kapital,** placing a necessary theoretical weapon in the hands of the workers' movement. In Volume One, Marx demonstrates that capitalism is based on the *exploitation* of working women, men, and children. All the basic facts of modern society are analysed, from prices and profits to wages and the working day. Why labour products are 'commodities,' why money is so all-powerful, where capital originates and why economic crises happen—all these Marx analyses with searching care.

20

Engels had, indeed, been busy promoting **Capital**, as had others in the International. Still, **Das Kapital** didn't sell very briskly at first. Karl's mother, **Henrietta,** complained:

(＊ THIS IS WHAT MARX ADVISED HIS FRIEND FRANZISKA KUGELMANN)

I n 1871, the PARIS COMMUNE took place! A spectacular uprising of Parisian workers and small independent producers had occurred during the Franco-Prussian war of 1870. Bitterly discontented with the repressive regime of the first emperor Napoleon's adventurer nephew, Louis Napoleon Bonaparte, the workers of Paris decided to take their lives into their own hands.

In March 1871 the Parisian working people toppled the government and seized the reins of power. By means of energetic, determined, and radically democratic measures, these working men and women reconstituted Paris as a socialist commune.

'THEY STORMED THE GATES OF HEAVEN. WHAT INITIATIVE, WHAT ELASTICITY, WHAT HEROISM THESE PARISIANS HAVE SHOWN!'

Speaking for the International, Marx declared the Paris Commune the first example of 'the dictatorship of the proletariat'. He meant the working class ruling itself democratically, in its own name, while fighting off the counter-revolutionary efforts of the displaced capitalist class.

' THE BEST THING ABOUT THE COMMUNE WAS ITS OWN WORKING EXISTENCE ITS DEMOCRATIC PROCEDURES, THE STEPS TAKEN TOWARDS THE ABOLITION OF PRIVATE PROPERTY, THE CREATION OF REAL WORKING COOPERATION BETWEEN PRODUCERS... '

But now something unusual in military annals took place. After two glorious months of the Commune, the French and Prussian armies—once at each other's throats—harbouring not the slightest tender feelings for one another—united to oppose the Parisian workers. Before long, the military effort to overwhelm the Commune met with success. A White Terror much more brutal than the terror of the French Revolution of 1793 followed. More than a hundred thousand Communards were killed. Thousands more were exiled.

'Paris has been delivered. At last the fighting is over; order work and security will reign once more.' Marshal MacMahon

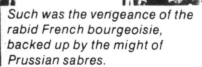

Such was the vengeance of the rabid French bourgeoisie, backed up by the might of Prussian sabres.

It was at this fateful juncture that Marx set about revising **Das Kapital** for a French translation. This appeared as a series of penny pamphlets, intended for Parisian working people, between 1872 and 1875.

Marx's French publisher, Lachâtre, was an exiled Communard. Marx's goal was to communicate his analysis of capitalism and the class struggle to the survivors of the Commune. He hoped that this would help them regroup and rethink their strategy.

Is **Das Kapital** an obscure, lifeless, esoteric work?

No.

Capital is for everyone who works for a living in the shadow of a boss. It argues that capitalism is a world system based on wage-labour. The relevance of Marx's **Capital** grows as wage-labour extends into all corners of the earth.

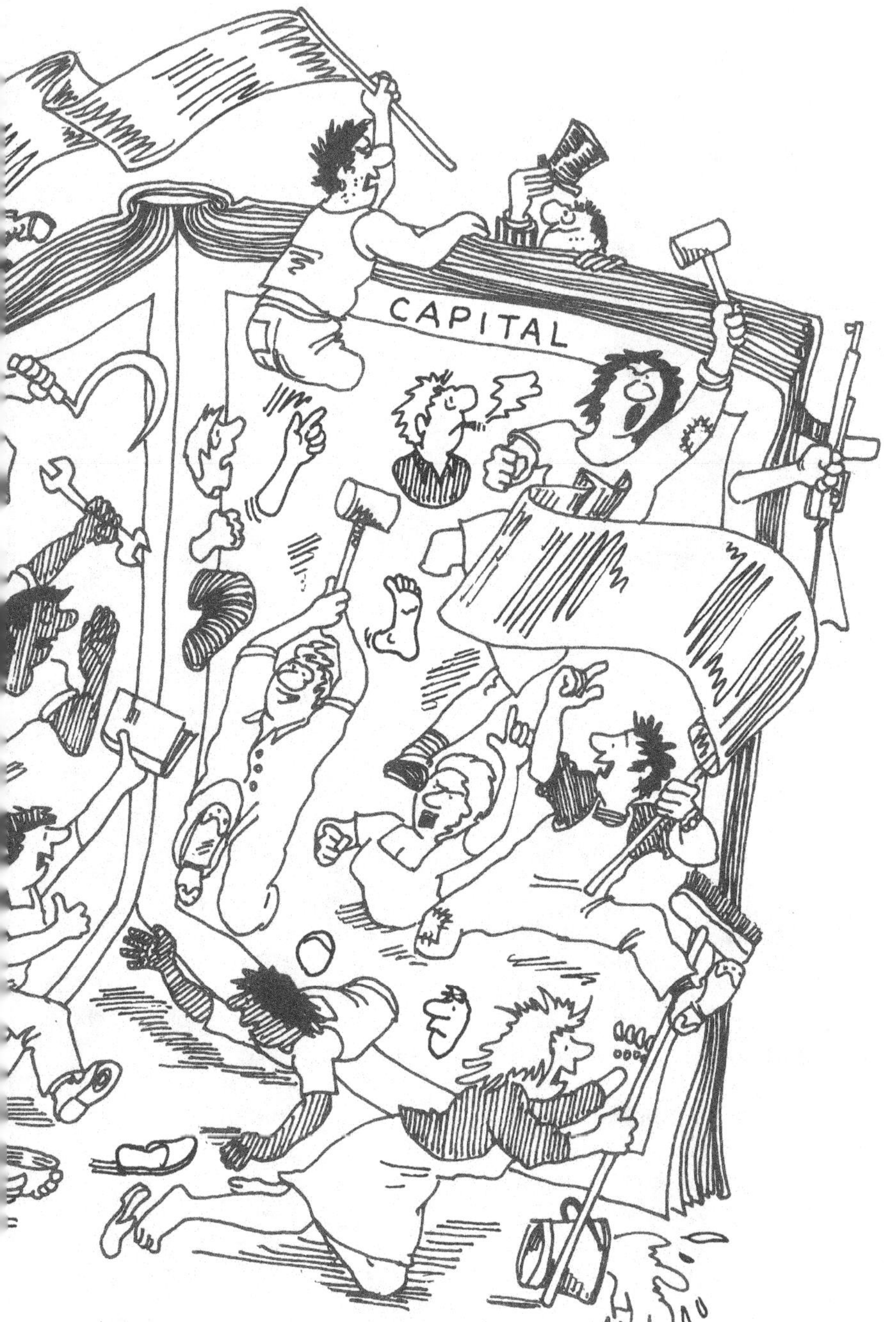
CAPITAL

1.
COMMODITIES

People *make* commodities; *sell* commodities; *buy* commodities. That's what the hustle and bustle is all about.

ANYTHING PRODUCED FOR EXCHANGE IS A COMMODITY!

Every day, on every side, we encounter an immense accumulation of commodities. All these worldly things—ready for sale, waiting to tempt money from our pockets are 'commodities', bearing odious, white paper labels with familiar symbols.

This is how commodities appear—with prices on their foreheads, talking dollars and cents. The price tag is the unique insignia of the commodity.

This accumulation of commodities; this mass of objects bearing price tags—this we may call THE WEALTH OF CAPITALIST SOCIETY.

£27

THE COMMODITY
AS AN ODDITY

The commodity is an oddity because it leads a *double life*.
It is a product of labour made not just for **use**, but for
exchange. 'For sale', the product acquires a quality not
present in nature—*exchangeability*. As a commodity, it is
not only *useful* but *exchangeable*.

Furs, for example, can be used either to protect us from the
cold—or to attract money. Spices can flavour our food—or
sell for a price. Here we have the unique feature of the
product as a commodity. It has two dimensions: both *what
it is*, and what it is *worth*. The commodity is not just an
object, but an object with a *price*.

29

In the language of the early economists, we may say with **Adam Smith,** that:

A Commodity if both a ufe value and a value!

GOODNESS ME — HOW DIFFICULT! AND ALL I WANTED WAS A PAIR OF SOCKS!

To grasp value we must fully understand the relationship between use-value and value.

Together, use-value and value are the twin sides of the commodity—they are the opposite poles of its double life.

'A use-value is anything outside us that we find necessary, useful, or pleasant. By the use of its properties, the useful thing allows us to satisfy some need or desire.'

There is surely no mystery here! As a useful product, the commodity is *not* an oddity. But the commodity is far more than a simple use-value.

A ROSE IS A ROSE IS A ROSE.

GERTRUDE STEIN

Materially useful as a use-value, the rose is *socially* useful *(exchangeable)* as a commodity. Fragrant and lovely, the rose also sells for a dollar, and trades for a handful of chocolates.

In a nutshell the commodity is valuable both for *use* and for *exchange*.

2. PRODUCTS FOR USE

Before capitalism began (in Europe in the 15th century) and even afterwards (until quite recently, in fact), production in most parts of the world was production for *use*. Dresses were made to be *worn*, not *sold*. Chocolates were made to be *eaten*, not *exchanged*. *Only with the ascent of capitalism did production for exchange become predominant.*

During the lifetime of Aristotle—circa 220 B.C.—commerce was a lively but very minor part of overall economic life. 'Economics', in fact, is the name Aristotle applied to production for use. Production for *exchange* Aristotle called 'Chrematistics.'

BRITISH MUSEUM

CHREMA-WOT-STICKS?

ARISTOTLE

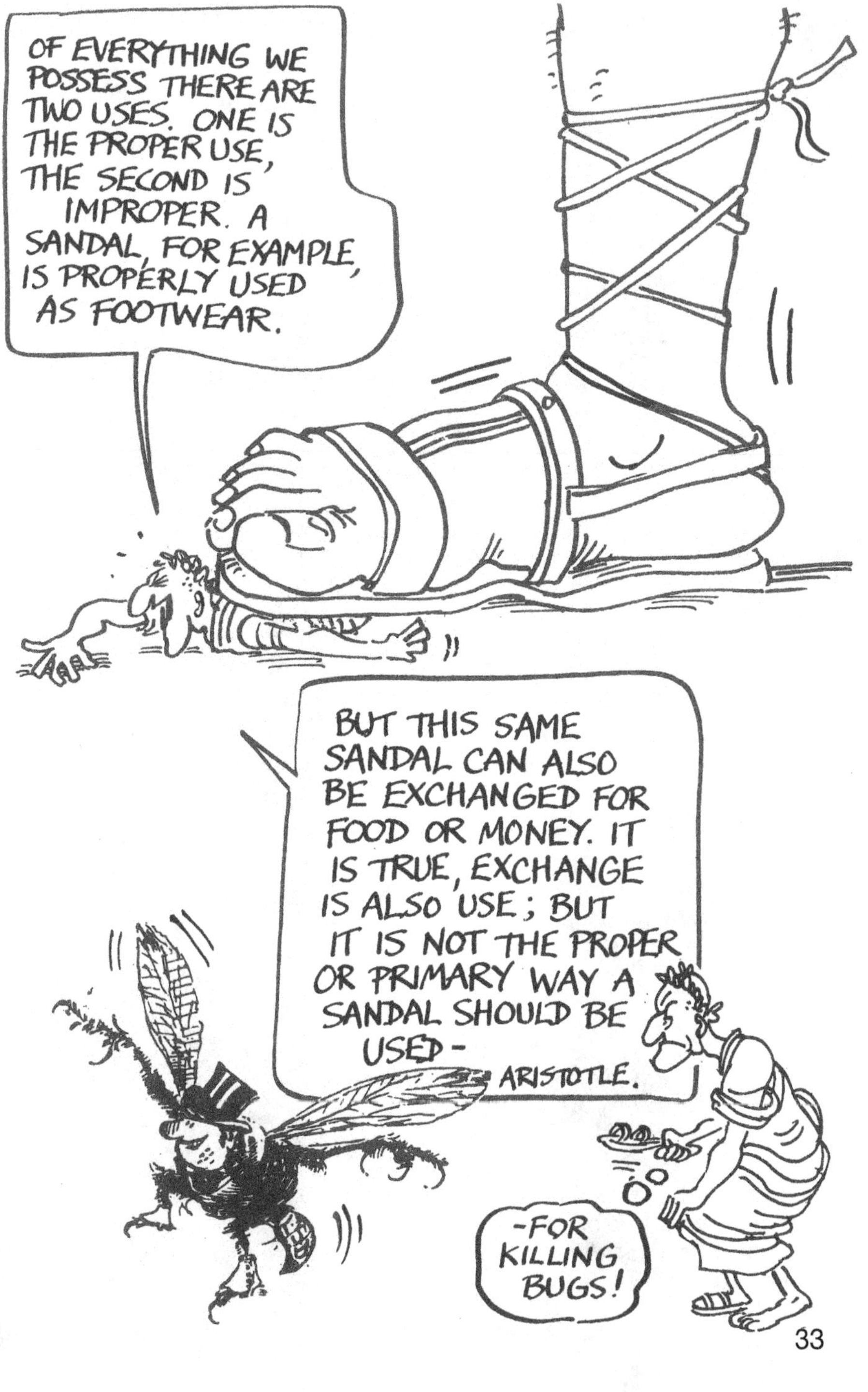
OF EVERYTHING WE POSSESS THERE ARE TWO USES. ONE IS THE PROPER USE, THE SECOND IS IMPROPER. A SANDAL, FOR EXAMPLE, IS PROPERLY USED AS FOOTWEAR.
BUT THIS SAME SANDAL CAN ALSO BE EXCHANGED FOR FOOD OR MONEY. IT IS TRUE, EXCHANGE IS ALSO USE; BUT IT IS NOT THE PROPER OR PRIMARY WAY A SANDAL SHOULD BE USED - ARISTOTLE.
-FOR KILLING BUGS!

The same was true for slaveholding antiquity—in Egypt, Greece, Carthage, Rome, and elsewhere. Though slaves produced for the use of *others*—their masters—they seldom produced for exchange. Nor were commodities typically produced by European serfs, Chinese peasants, Indian patriarchal families, or working people of other pre-capitalist societies.

Use-value, not exchange-value, was the goal and result of pre-capitalist production. Indeed, producing to *sell* and *profit* was typically regarded as immoral, a perverse way of life inspired by greed, pride, gluttony, and vanity.

Only in capitalist society does exchangeability become an established feature of the labour product. *Only in capitalist society, thus, does the product lead a double life—as a value and a use-value.*

3. ALIENATION OF USE-VALUE

If we are fully to grasp capitalist production, we must recognize, above all, that the double life of the commodity is neither peaceful nor harmonious. On the contrary, value and use-value clash. The capitalist quest for profit—for ever greater sums of value—radically clashes with human desires for food, shelter, and other use-values.

THE CAPITALIST QUEST FOR PROFIT FOREVER-GREATER SUMS OF VALUE CLASHES WITH HUMAN DESIRES FOR FOOD, SHELTER, AND OTHER USE-VALUES

We are speaking now of the distortion, repression, and abuse of the product as a useful object—its misuse as *use-value*. To the extent that the product is treated as a value, it is *alienated* as a use-value.

A commodity must *be* or *seem* useful if anyone is to buy it. But usefulness is not the only issue, or even the main issue, for a product that is treated and regarded as a commodity. As such, the product must be *sold* in order to be *used*.

Sale is the indispensable prerequisite for use. Without exchange, there can be no use. If a commodity fails to prove its saleability, its usefulness withers on the vine.

I CALL IT "THE WHEEL."
NOW ALL I NEED IS A BOAT...
AND A MARKET.

Thus does 'unnatural' exchange get in the way of 'natural' use.

Take a loaf of bread, for example. Sitting in a supermarket, its usefulness lies completely dormant. Though perfectly edible, it must prove its *exchange-value* before it can be eaten. If no one buys it, the bread will rot on the shelf—even though people starve.

The same is true for every commodity: NO SALE, NO USE. This is a principle of private property. Commodities are not made to be given away. Capitalists do not share with workers.

Another example of the distortion of use-value resulting from production for exchange is the *sabotage* of the product. Business cares about product quality only from the standpoint of sales. If sales are unaffected, business will happily cut costs by skimping on labour, safety precautions and materials, —typically making useless, dangerous, even deadly products. Are the following horrors unfamiliar?

- Cars 'unsafe at any speed'

- Baby formulas poisonous to infants

- Food shot up with carcinogens

- Nuclear power plants with sub-standard insulation·

- Medicine that kills

- Unsafe chemical plants

- Products contaminated with asbestos, mercury, etc.

And so it goes.

38

4. OVERPRODUCTION

Still another example of how exchange-value eclipses use-value is evident in so-called 'over-production'. Periodically, production results in what business regards as an 'excess' of commodities. The consequence is that prices and profits fall—to the chagrin and mortal fury of capitalists. The market, they say, is 'glutted'. To reverse matters, business intentionally and cheerfully destroys part of its product. Why? Simply to raise prices and profits. Never mind that people lack adequate housing, medical care, or food. From the profit-standpoint of business, the market 'glut' is a catastrophe. It must

be disposed of. *Not* by making surplus use-values freely *available* to people—heavens, no! Rather, by *destroying* them.

'SURPLUS' TOMATOES BEING BURNED IN THE U.S.

This is what happened, for example, during the Great Depression of the 1930s. Agribusiness found itself burdened with an 'excess' of pigs and milk causing prices to fall.

The result was that pigs were killed and milk was spilled, in vast quantities, to safeguard profits--though many were hungry. To keep profits *up*, supply is kept *down*.

Production is restricted as a matter of course.

In the US, for example, barely 70% of the total productive capacity is used. Much of the general production apparatus remains idle--to say nothing of the millions of unemployed workers.

As we see, capitalism requires products universally endowed with exchangeability. Business places a premium not on what the object is, but on its *value*-- what it *sells for*.

EMPLOYMENT OFFICE

YOU MUST BE NEW HERE OR YOU'D KNOW THAT'S WHERE I USUALLY LEAN!

5. If value exists and appears only in exchange, it is imperative for us to grasp the meaning of exchange. Aristotle is once again a helpful guide.

CONSIDER AN EXCHANGE OF FIVE BEDS FOR ONE HOUSE. THESE PRODUCTS ARE NOT ALIKE. BEDS AND HOUSES HAVE DIFFERENT QUALITIES AND DIFFERENT USES. HOW, THEN, CAN THEY EXCHANGE AS EQUALS? ARE THEY REALLY EQUAL?

NO! THOUGH EXCHANGING THEM SEEMS TO IMPLY THEIR EQUALITY, BEDS AND HOUSES ARE NOT REALLY EQUAL. THE APPEARANCE OF EQUALITY IS FALSE. IN REALITY, PEOPLE SIMPLY DECIDE TO EXCHANGE UNEQUAL THINGS.

However, Aristotle ultimately came to the conclusion that real equality between commodities is impossible. After all, Aristotle reasoned, no two objects are really the same. Though mistaken in his conclusion, Aristotle at least seriously grappled with the problem of 'equality' in exchange. This elevates him head and shoulders above most contemporary economists, who refuse even to consider the possibility that exchange embodies an inherent principle of equality.

That *just so much* (not more, not less) is the price of a commodity when supply and demand balance indicates that something else is the basis for this price.

THIS 'SOMETHING ELSE' —I MAINTAIN— IS LABOUR!

YOU'RE STANDING ON MY FOOT!

If we agree with Aristotle that no two objects are exactly alike—and if they were, why would we exchange them?— we face a difficulty. How can objects that are materially unlike, with unlike properties, systematically exchange for each other in established proportions?

Imagine for a moment that there are just two objects in question—say, a deer and a beaver—and just two owners (both of them hunters). Suppose that it requires one day of hunting to capture a deer, but seven days to capture a beaver. If both hunters are equally skilful at catching both types of quarry, then parting with one beaver for one deer seems unreasonable. Why trade the product of seven day's labour for the product of one day's labour? Why hunt for seven days to wind up with a deer requiring only one day of hunting?

It *is* possible to make this exchange—what would prevent it? Any producer can make an unequal exchange either unwittingly or if s/he so desires. But the matter changes when we talk about *systematic* commodity exchange, that is, capitalism. Here, the principle that regulates commodity exchange is *labour-time.* Materially, commodities may be totally dissimilar—but they do have one thing in common: all require human effort for their production or appropriation. This provides a basis for exchange.

By this standard, seven deer are equal to one beaver. That is, each embodies an equal quantity of labour.

This raises a problem: what does it mean to say that a product 'embodies'labor?

Just this: that so much labour 'goes into' the product. In production, the material object existing before production changes. The body of the object changes with the labour expended upon it. This labour thus has 'bodily' results—it is *embodied* in a material thing.

Before work begins, the object already has a particular form derived from nature. Labour *adds* to this, changing the form of the object. In this way, the purpose guiding labour is 'objectified'—it *goes into* the object.

43

6. ABSTRACT LABOUR

A moment ago, we said that the basis for comparison between different commodities is the amount of labour required for each. But a problem arises: what *kind* of labour are we referring to? If useful labour adds to the *usefulness* of the product—what makes it *exchangeable*? What type of labour makes a rose, for instance, a *commodity*? Useful labour?

No. That was **David Ricardo's** mistake. Brilliantly perceiving that value is *embodied labour,* Ricardo failed fully to analyse this proposition. Above all, Ricardo fell short of the concept of *abstract* labour ...

Though different kinds of labour are not materially equal, they can be *treated as if they were.* This is vital! This is the secret we've been seeking.

Materially unequal different forms of useful labour— say, watchmaking and bed-making—can be *treated as if they were equal,* to facilitate exchange. Activities involving different skills, different operations, and different tools can be treated as the *same*—so that the products of different activities can be regarded as equal.

In other words: USEFUL LABOUR can be treated as ABSTRACT LABOUR.

A USEFUL RICARDO

AN ABSTRACT RICARDO

Before exploring abstract labour in detail, it will be useful
to draw a preliminary contrast:

USEFUL LABOUR

Work activities as they
really are with unique
material qualities

Embodied in use-value

ABSTRACT LABOUR

Work activities *treated* as if
they had *no* distinguishing
qualities

Embodied in value

THERE IS NO ROYAL ROAD TO SCIENCE, AND ONLY THOSE WHO DO NOT DREAD THE FATIGUING CLIMB OF ITS STEEP PATHS HAVE A CHANCE OF GAINING ITS LUMINOUS SUMMITS. MY CONCEPT OF VALUE, IN PARTICULAR, REQUIRES SERIOUS STUDY.

BECAUSE IT'S THERE!

DAMN! I'VE DROPPED THE GRUNDRISSE!

When tailors and weavers exchange products, for example, they view their work not as it really is, but as work, pure and simple, as labour *per se*. Equating one coat to 20 yds of linen means equating *coatmaking* (the labour of a tailor) to *linenmaking* (the labour of a weaver). The *products* are equated—and so is the labour that *goes into* them. *Trading products* means *treating* them as *equal*.

Sans qualities, all labour is *alike.* X hours of one type of quality-less labour is equal to X hours of another type of quality-less labour. Thus, abstractness permits exchange. Equal quantities of abstract labour may exchange for one another. With the fact of exchange itself, abstract labour is certified as real. The product proves itself to be a commodity, an embodiment of value.

47

 =

Producers don't usually think to themselves 'Aha! By trading my watch for a bed, I simultaneously disregard the material qualities of both products, viewing them as qualitatively equal and thus rendering them the result not of useful but of abstract labour.'

But this is what people do .... whatever they may think.

When a palace is traded for so many tins of boot polish, the labour embodied in each is treated, *de facto,* as if it were identical to the other. The same is true when a volume of

Shakespeare's works is exchanged for so many ounces of snuff. Clearly, the use-value of each product differs—and so does the useful labour corresponding to this use-value. *They are values.*

This means that the qualitatively *unequal* useful labour embodied in them is treated as qualitatively equal. When we exchange watches, dresses, beds or houses we disregard their material properties. The basis for this is that we disregard the material differences between *watchmaking, dressmaking, bed-making* and *house-building.* A certain number of watches—made of metal, jewels, and glass—are exchangeable for a certain number of beds—made of goosefeathers, wood, foam rubber and cloth—because the different kinds of *labour* required to assemble them *are treated as equal.*

It isn't that two kinds of labour lurk in the body of the commodity. Rather, the *useful* labour inherent in the product as a use-value can be treated as qualitatively abstract to facilitate exchange.

No matter how slowly you work, the commodity you produce contains only the amount of 'equal' labour-time that the *average* producer would expend. If you try to charge a price for your product on the basis of the exact, actual time it takes, you will soon discover that the *actual* time spent performing useful labour is not the point. It's how much socially *standard* labour— *abstract* labour—the product normally requires.

Average, equal labour is what people pay attention to—and it can change suddenly, for reasons independent of the nature of concrete, useful labour.

49

When the power-loom was introduced into England, for example, it halved the time required to make cloth. Hand-loom weavers, unable to afford power-looms, now found their product just half as valuable as before—not because their own, actual labour had changed, but because the level of socially standard labour had changed.

BEFORE THE INTRODUCTION OF THE POWER LOOM, HAND LOOM WEAVERS WENT AROUND WITH £5 NOTES STUCK IN THEIR HATBANDS.

AFTERWARDS THEY WENT ROUND 'WITH HATS ...

So it should be very clear that 'equal' labour is not *real, material* labour, but real labour regarded as *socially abstract* labour.

7. ALIENATION OF USEFUL LABOUR

If, as we have said, every commodity 'contains' or 'embodies' abstract LABOUR—where is it to be found? Take a coat, for example. Is the abstract LABOUR in the lining, in the sleeves, in the collar? No. No matter how threadbare and ragged this coat may become, the abstract LABOUR it contains can never be materially found.

So far, no chemist has ever discovered value in a watch, a coat, or any other commodity. Look at the watch under a microscope! Through a telescope! Turn it upside down, inside out, examine it as you will—no matter what you do, you will never see, hear, touch or taste value. All you will actually see is the thing itself—in this case, the watch. And you will never see or hear an actual living person engaged in abstract labour.

Only useful things and useful labour can be discerned by the senses. *Since value is not material, it cannot be materially perceived.* It is social, a ghostly social reality. "The value of commodities is the very opposite of the coarse materiality of their bodies, not an atom of matter enters into it."

JUST AS A KING IS REALLY A KING —AS A RESULT OF SOCIAL PRACTICE!

A king is a man like any other man, that is, different from all others—in manner, looks and temperament.

You can't tell by looking at him that he's king—he appears to be just a man. But the monarch is treated as a king. He may not possess the 'Divine Right' imputed to him, but, because his subjects treat him royally, he is a king. He has 'kingly powers'.

Kingly powers and qualities are social, not natural. No coroner examining a king's dead body would discover a trace of royalty in his blood. (It isn't blue).

Naturally, materially, the king is just a man. His material powers are just human powers. But socially, in his activities, in the way people respond to him, the king is what his subjects imagine him to be.

People make him a king by treating him as one.

So it is with value. No useful object materially embodies abstract LABOUR.

A useful object can be a commodity—an embodiment of value—only be being *treated* as a commodity. But if it is treated as a commodity, then it *becomes* a commodity—*socially*.

YOU CANNOT TELL BY LOOKING AT A DIAMOND THAT IT IS A COMMODITY. WHERE IT SERVES AS AN AESTHETIC OR MECHANICAL USE-VALUE, ON THE BREAST OF A COURTESAN OR IN THE HAND OF A GLASS-CUTTER, IT IS A DIAMOND, AND NOT A COMMODITY.

In nature, there are no commodities. Just try to find value in Davy Jones' locker, or at the centre of the earth, or in outer space. Indeed, nothing is 'exchangeable' where there are no people. Exchange is an act of human relations. Exchangeability is a property possible only in the context of human social relations. But though unnatural, exchangeability can exist. *People* can make useful things exchangeable—by producing for exchange.

When exchange becomes the universal, systematic principle of production—as it is in capitalist society—then exchangeability becomes a socially real attribute of products in general. 'Ghostly' value is very, very real. Try to survive in capitalist society without buying or selling things!

With minor exceptions, *everyone* in capitalist society buys and sells commodities.

8. Fetishism

The word **fetishism** denotes the belief that particular objects -- say, religious idols or gold bars -- have mystical powers.

A **fetish** is precisely such an object.

Stemming from the Latin word for "making," the word **fetish** refers to a man-made object that observers interpret as the host of a supernatural power, whether sacred or demonic.

Modern critics, beginning with De Brosses and Comte, saw fetishism as a stage in the history of religions. So it is today, Marx says, with the fetishism inherent in the world of commodities -- **commodity fetishism**.

This is the belief that labor products possess, besides ordinary material traits, invisible but inherent *'exchange value'*...

Commodities appear to relate to each other naturally and spontaneously...

What really happens is that society divides its labour between a multitude of 'private producers,' who relate to each other by exchanging their products. It is this process which transforms simple use-values into magical values.

Though commodities and money do have special powers, these powers are not natural. This is, however, what people imagine. Seldom is it realised that money and commodities only have the power of exchangeability because people relate to each other as private producers. Producing in isolation from others working 'privately', producers *must* produce for exchange.

Only by exchange can products change hands. Without exchange, a private apple grower would have—only apples! To get wine, books, shoes, and other products, producers must burst from the shell of their privacy at least long enough for exchange to take place.

No one producer can use indefinite quantities of any one use-value. Beyond a certain point, the producer's product becomes a *non-use-value* for the producer, something of redeeming value only in exchange—where it appeals to some other producer as a use-value.

The appearance is that apples exchange for money (and thus, indirectly, for wine, books, and so on) *naturally*, as an expression of their inborn exchangeability. Commodities seem to attract money just as a magnet attracts iron. It seems natural for commodities to have particular prices; to be 'worth' just so much, no more and no less. This is fetishism.

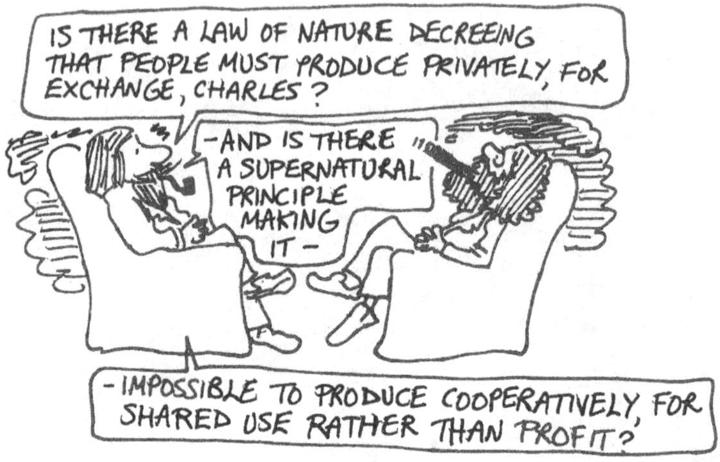
IS THERE A LAW OF NATURE DECREEING THAT PEOPLE MUST PRODUCE PRIVATELY, FOR EXCHANGE, CHARLES?
-AND IS THERE A SUPERNATURAL PRINCIPLE MAKING IT -
- IMPOSSIBLE TO PRODUCE COOPERATIVELY, FOR SHARED USE RATHER THAN PROFIT?

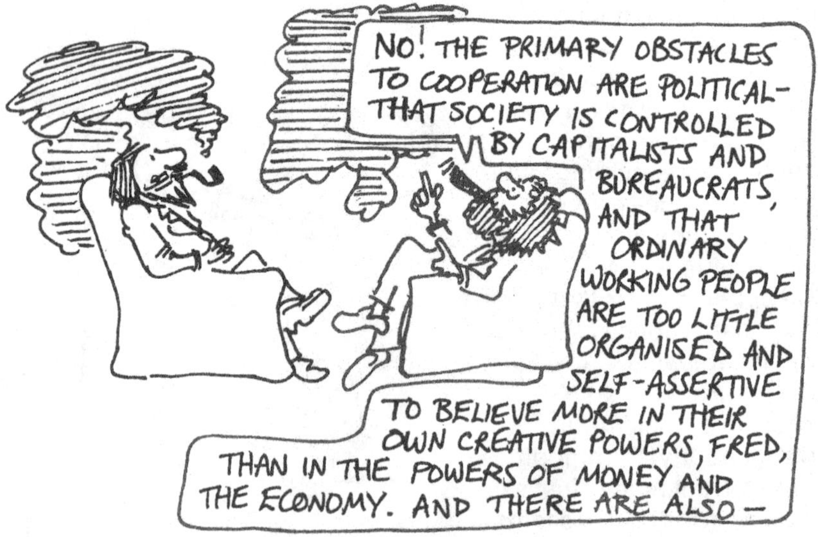
NO! THE PRIMARY OBSTACLES TO COOPERATION ARE POLITICAL - THAT SOCIETY IS CONTROLLED BY CAPITALISTS AND BUREAUCRATS, AND THAT ORDINARY WORKING PEOPLE ARE TOO LITTLE ORGANISED AND SELF-ASSERTIVE TO BELIEVE MORE IN THEIR OWN CREATIVE POWERS, FRED, THAN IN THE POWERS OF MONEY AND THE ECONOMY. AND THERE ARE ALSO -

- PSYCHOLOGICAL BARRIERS. PEOPLE, REARED UNDER CAPITALISM, ACQUIRE AN INGRAINED WILLINGNESS TO TAKE ORDERS, TO BOW DOWN BEFORE AUTHORITY! MANY ACQUIRE A VESTED EMOTIONAL STAKE IN ALL TYPES OF AUTHORITARIAN RELATIONS — MEN DOMINATING WOMEN, ONE NATION DOMINATING ANOTHER, ONE RACE OPPRESSING ANOTHER, HIGHER LEVELS OF THE WORKFORCE LORDING IT OVER LOWER LEVELS... AND THE MOST PROFOUND QUESTION OF REVOLUTIONARY WORKING CLASS POLITICS IS WHETHER OR NOT THESE BARRIERS CAN BE — WILL BE — OVERCOME...

- IS THAT CLEAR?

9. MONEY

Value exists in three forms: as *commodities*, *money*, and *capital*.

•**COMMODITIES are use-values produced for exchange.**

•**MONEY is the universal commodity, equivalent to all others.**

•**CAPITAL is money invested to generate more money**

To discuss *capital*, the very highest form of value, we must better understand money. How does money emerge from the exchange of commodities? How does money come to dominate the exchange of commodities as capital?

60

In the simplest case—where a single commodity is exchanged for just one equivalent commodity—the value-relation is not well established. Deciding how much 'socially average' labour is required to produce this or that is mostly a matter of guesswork. But when products are *generally* produced for exchange, value-relations grow more established. When one coat= 20 metres of linen = 10 kilos of tea = 40 kilos of coffee = 20 grammes of gold, exchange ratios become more fixed, less haphazard. Ever more products are treated as units of abstract labour. Finally, a system of commodity production arises, in which the relative value magnitudes of the different commodities are systematically fixed.

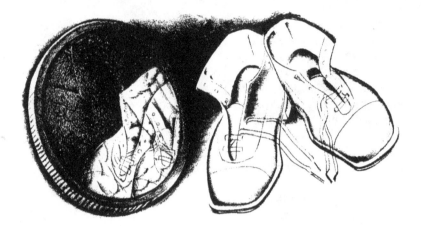

When one relative commodity is confronted not by one equivalent commodity, but by many, its value is expressed independently by an array of equivalents. But turn the situation around. We can also say that each commodity in this array of equivalents views the 'one relative' commodity as *itself* an equivalent. If this one commodity is used to express the value of many—it becomes *money*. It plays the role of money most fully when it is recognised universally as the one equivalent commodity, expressing—and measuring—the value of all others.

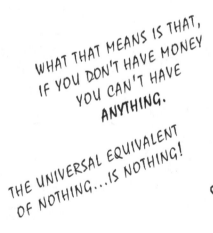

WHAT THAT MEANS IS THAT, IF YOU DON'T HAVE MONEY YOU CAN'T HAVE **ANYTHING.**

THE UNIVERSAL EQUIVALENT OF NOTHING...IS NOTHING!

GOLD

Historically, *gold* has been the particular commodity most universally used as money. With the rise of the 'gold standard', it became appropriate to say not that 1 coat = 20 metres of linen, but that 1 coat = $15 and that 20 metres of linen = $15. Coat and linen can still be exchanged, but it is now customary to use *money* to effect the trade. The equivalence of the coat and linen is expressed, not directly, but by their common relationship to gold (using one of its money-names—$, £, etc.). Gold emerges as the power of powers when it becomes the single commodity uniquely exchangeable for all others. Coats and linen can now buy *only* money. The same is true for all ordinary commodities (with trivial exceptions).

But gold—
and its paper, copper, and other representatives—can buy *any* and *every* other commodity. This is what makes it money, and sets it apart from all other commodities.

63

The playwright Ben Jonson conveyed a sharp sense of the real social power of money when he spoke of

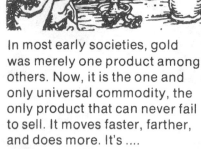

RICHES - THE DUMB GOD THAT GIV'ST ALL MEN TONGUES, THAT CAN'ST DO NAUGHT, AND YET MAK'ST MEN DO ALL THINGS!

'THE ALCHEMIST'

In most early societies, gold was merely one product among others. Now, it is the one and only universal commodity, the only product that can never fail to sell. It moves faster, farther, and does more. It's ....

SUPERCOMMODITY!!

And its powers are multiplied more than ever when it functions as capital.

As capital, money does indeed 'mak'st men do all things.'

10. THE ACCUMULATION OF CAPITAL

WHEN WE SPEAK OF CAPITALISM, WE SPEAK NOT JUST OF MONEY, BUT OF MONEY GAIN—OF MONEY INVESTED AS CAPITAL TO GENERATE PROFIT!

What is profit, and where does it originate? If an entrepreneur starts with a given sum of money, how does an extra sum enter his pocket? If we start with a given sum of value, where does surplus value come from?

How does this work?

Take our friend Lessner, a hired tailor; his father, a self-employed tailor; and Moneybags, a capitalist.

Each relates to money in a different way.

Both Lessner and his father sell in order to buy. One sells the *ability* to make coats (Lessner) and the other sells coats (Lessner's father). Both seek specific, needed commodities.

The father makes and sells coats not for money as an end in itself, but as a means to obtain food, shelter, and other commodities.

WHAT IS THE DIFFERENCE BETWEEN A WELL-DRESSED MAN AND A TIRED DOG?

The same is true for friend Lessner—he sells his ability to work not for love, but for money; for wages, as a means to obtain life's necessities.

THE MAN WEARS AN ENTIRE SUIT, THE DOG JUST PANTS.

What we see here is the cycle C-M-C, COMMODITIES - MONEY - COMMODITIES, where Money is a step on the path from *making* Commodities to *buying* Commodities

It is different with friend Moneybags. He enters the scene not as a direct producer, but as a *money-owner*. His goal is to buy commodities to sell them. He spends money to get money.

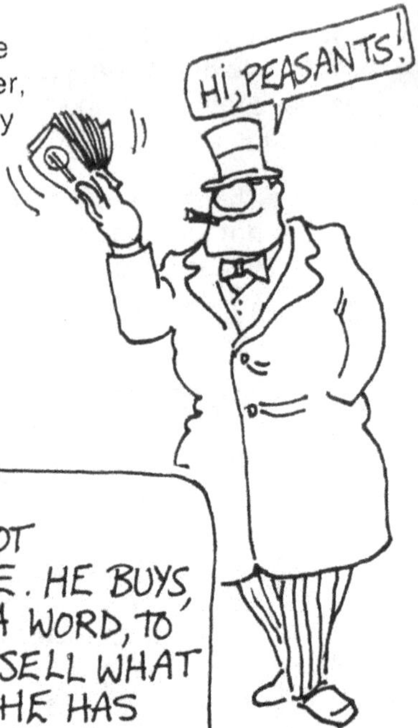
HI, PEASANTS!

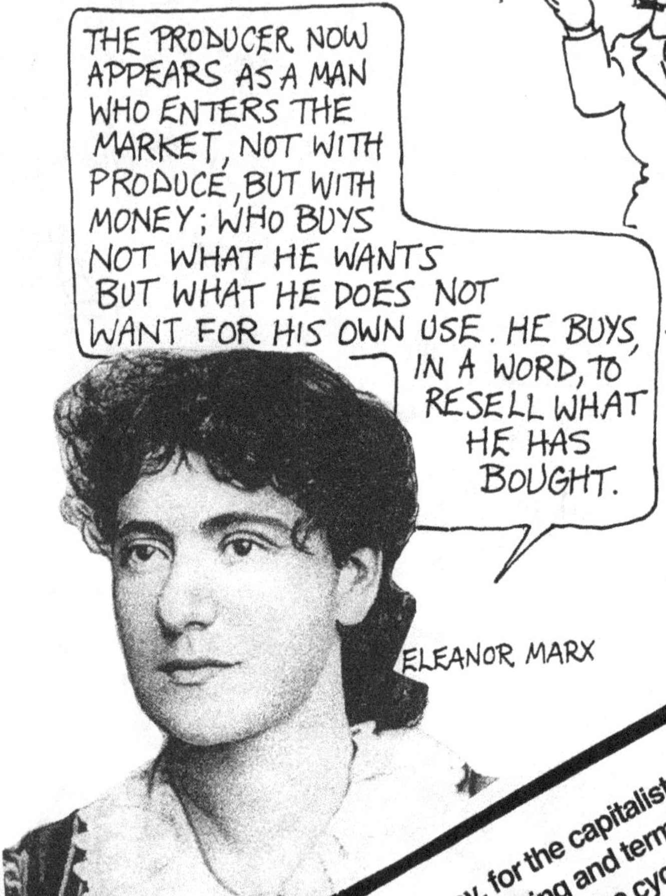
THE PRODUCER NOW APPEARS AS A MAN WHO ENTERS THE MARKET, NOT WITH PRODUCE, BUT WITH MONEY; WHO BUYS NOT WHAT HE WANTS BUT WHAT HE DOES NOT WANT FOR HIS OWN USE. HE BUYS, IN A WORD, TO RESELL WHAT HE HAS BOUGHT.
ELEANOR MARX

Money, for the capitalist, is the beginning and terminus of exchange. The cycle in which Moneybags lives is the reverse of C-M-C:

MONEY - COMMODITIES - MONEY

Moneybags spends money not merely to reap an equal sum of money. He does not invest 10 merely to get 10 back.

No, Moneybags aims to get more money than he spends -- to profit from exchange.

CHEESE!

I NEED MORE

CHEESE!

A victim of 'the accursed hunger for gold,' Moneybags finds himself on a passionate chase after value, a boundless quest for enrichment.

Why?

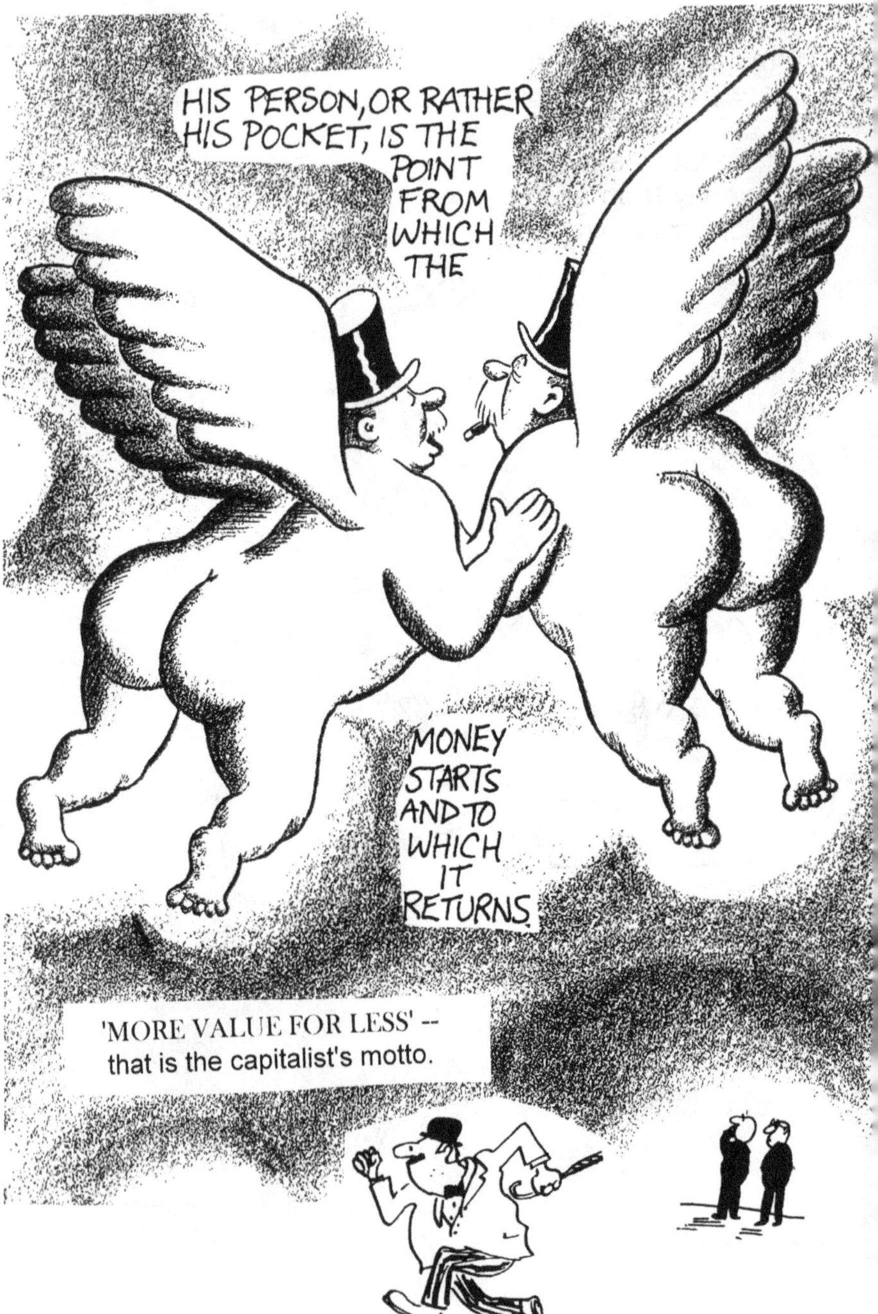
HIS PERSON, OR RATHER HIS POCKET, IS THE POINT FROM WHICH THE
MONEY STARTS AND TO WHICH IT RETURNS
'MORE VALUE FOR LESS' -- that is the capitalist's motto.

The miracle of money is that, properly used, it does produce profit. Money makes money! An *initial* sum of money, M, gives rise to an *expanded* sum of money, M^1 (pronounced **M-prime).**

Not simply M-C-M, then, but M-C-M$'$ is the capitalist's cycle, where M$'$ is greater than M. It is here that we find the origin of *surplus value*—the difference between M$'$ and M. An original sum of money is replaced by an expanded sum of value. Moneybags actually achieves 'more value for less.'

Money used to generate money is 'self-expanding value', or *capital*. We speak now of the initial M. Once invested, capital gives rise to surplus value, the difference between M and M′. This surplus value takes three basic forms: **profit, interest** and **rent**.

A portion of surplus value pays the interest on M—since it is likely that Moneybags borrows at least part of the initial capital. Another portion of surplus value is used to pay rent—since it is likely that Moneybags rents at least part of the land or equipment he uses.

What remains is *profit* -- surplus value that accrues directly to Moneybags, to use as he pleases.

I'll have a crate of escargot... oh, and two Picassos to go!

PRINCESS MIDIA
'AS GOOD AS GOLD'

Profit can be used in two basic ways -- either as *dividends*, for Moneybag's personal pleasure, or as *capital* -- as *fresh M, a second generation of M,* invested anew to generate another round of surplus value.

IF WE SUBTRACT INTEREST, RENT AND DIVIDENDS FROM M' WE ARE LEFT WITH A NEW M. IF THIS M — WHICH WE CAN DESIGNATE M2 — IS GREATER THAN THE ORIGINAL M THEN CAPITAL HAS ACCUMULATED!

Though the wealth of capitalist society presents itself as an accumulation of commodities, it is, in reality, an accumulation of *capital*. Capital accumulation is the defining principle of capitalism, the economic goal and process besides which all others pale into insignificance. Capitalism is just the nickname for the system of production based on the accumulation of capital.

As we have seen, profit-making is the means by which capital accumulates. Profit keeps the system going—like wind in the sails of a boat, or uranium in a nuclear reactor.

Money has *proven* its capacity to expand itself. Like the goose that lays the golden egg, money has shown that it possesses the occult power to add value to itself. Money begets money. 'The rich get richer'.
As capital, money tends to accumulate when invested. Profits are made.

Patting himself on the back, Moneybags characteristically says that profits result from 'buying cheap and selling dear', that is, *exchange*.

BUY CHEAP

—AND SELL DEAR

—PROFITS PILE UP ALL YEAR!

BUT BUY DEAR

—AND SELL CHEAP

—END UP ON THE RUBBISH HEAP!

Suppose that Moneybags sells his commodities above their value. He sells what is worth 100 for 110—thus adding a surcharge of 10. But what prevents all other sellers from doing the same? If this should happen, our friend Moneybags is at a loss—what he *gains* as a seller he *loses* as a buyer.

Swindling and shady dealing are rampant, of course. But, *in general*, overcharging for products is disallowed by competition. Rivalry between competing capitalists for limited markets and profits tends to keep prices hovering in the vicinity of value. The result is that commodities tend to sell for what they cost in terms of average, socially required labour.

76

Moneybags would of course like to overcharge for his products—but if he does, his competitors will cut into his sales by 'underselling' him. What Moneybags gains with his surcharge he loses in sales—if he isn't driven out of business altogether.

SURPRISING EFFECT OF COMPETITION

Consider, finally, one particular instance of swindling. Suppose that Mr A is ingenious enough to take advantage of Messrs. B and C. Fine—but will this produce surplus value? No! Some gain may occur, but this is at the expense of the gentlemen swindled. No *new* value is created.

VALUE HAS CHANGED HANDS, BUT IT HAS NOT BEEN CREATED, AND PROFITS—TO BE REAL—MUST BE NEWLY CREATED. IT IS SELF-EVIDENT THAT CAPITAL IS NOT PRODUCED BY CHEATING

ELEANOR MARX

When monopolies enter the picture, it changes somewhat—but not fundamentally. Though it *is* possible for monopolists to raise prices above values, unconstrained by competition and thus free to reap 'windfall' profits, profits, in general, are not the result of monopoly.

Without monopoly, even when production is perfectly competitive, profit is still the name of the game. The accumulation of capital started, remember, on the basis of competition. So we must look elsewhere for an explanation of profit ....

WE WORKERS DON'T SEE ANY OF THE PROFITS—

—HOWEVER BZZZY WE ARE—

—THEY HIVE THEM OFF FOR THE QUEEN—

—AND THE OTHER DRONES!

Capital is created not merely in exchange, as a *by-product* of buying and selling, but in production. *Between M and M' there is a process of production.* It is to this that we must turn if we are to grasp the origin of capital.

Q: WHAT POWER DOES MONEY HAVE?
A: JUST M–C, THE POWER TO BUY COMMODITIES.
Q: BUT M–C, WE HAVE SEEN, DOES NOT
   CREATE SURPLUS VALUE. WHAT DOES?
A: THE ACTION OF COMMODITIES IN
   PRODUCTION.
Q: EH ????!!?

More happens in M-C-M′ than exchange. Moneybags does not simply re-sell the very same commodities he buys. On the contrary, Moneybags buys commodities which give rise to new commodities.

If the value of the commodities produced is no greater than the value of the commodities purchased, Moneybags will make no profit. So Moneybags must be lucky enough to find a special commodity on the market which, once purchased, can be used to generate surplus value.
As it happens, Moneybags is in luck! He does find a special, value-creating commodity on the market.

11. LABOUR-POWER

Where money is the supercommodity, human labour-power is the SUPER supercommodity. Money buying labour power for the generation of surplus value is what capitalism is all about. Only by purchasing labour power can money act as capital—and only in this way can capital be accumulated.

Capitalism ultimately depends on the commodification of labour-power. But how? By what historical process did the human capacity for labour become 'commodified'? By what process did direct producers becomes proletarians, sellers of labour-power, *workers*?

— A SHORT HISTORY. A FULLER ONE COMES LATER...

PLAGUE.

PUBLICK NOTICE
YOU'VE
ALL
HADDETH
IT

INDUSTRIAL
REVOLUTION.

WAR.

GOOD LUCK
OLD CHAP!

LEISURE.

10 bn.
JOBLESS

'We know by experience that a relatively feeble development of commodity circulation suffices for the creation of money. But capital requires more than the mere circulation of money and commodities. Capital arises only when the money-owner, as the owner of factories, tools, etc., finds the free worker available on the market as the seller of labour-power. This one historical precondition comprises a world's history. Capital arises on this basis, announcing a new epoch in social production.'

'But how are we to explain this strange phenomenon—that we find on the market a set of buyers (owning money, land, and machinery) and a set of sellers (owning nothing but labour-power, their working arms and brains)? How does it come about that one class buys continually to make profits and grow rich, while the working class continually sells its labour-power just to earn a livelihood?'

CONGRATULATIONS! IT'S A CAPITALIST! SEE THE LITTLE SPOON?

UNLUCKY. IT'S A WORKER!

One thing is clear. Nature does not produce capitalists, on the one hand, and workers, on the other.

Social classes don't fall from the sky, or leap fully-formed from the earth. The bourgeoisie—the ruling class—and the proletariat—the working class—in particular, resulted from a long chain of historical developments.

12. EXPROPRIATION

THIS PROCESS OF HISTORY I CALL 'THE ORIGINAL EXPROPRIATION OF THE PRODUCER', THE SERIES OF EVENTS AND STRUGGLES BY WHICH PRODUCERS WERE DIVORCED FROM THE MEANS OF PRODUCTION.

The means of production are crucial. These include implements, machinery, buildings, raw materials, resources, and all other items required for production. Production as such is the active combination of human energy—labour-power—and production resources—means of production.

When production resources are controlled by direct producers, labour-power and means of production combine organically. Take small farmers, growing wheat, or artisans, making hats. Directly in possession of the needed tools and materials of their trades, these direct producers simply *make use* of production resources. The resulting production is independent, and self-sufficient.

'But take away the land—the livestock—the energy resources. Wrench the tools from the producer's hands, and what is left? An uprooted vagabond, whose only possession is labour-power.'

This expropriation of the producer is precisely the historical precondition for capitalism. Formerly united, means of production and labour-power are now sundered. The capitalist takes possession of the means of production. Without means of production, the direct producer has nothing—except labour-power. To survive, the producer must sell his or her labour-power for wages, thus becoming a proletarian.

THERE MUST BE AN EASIER WAY TO MAKE A LIVING...

In this way, labour-power and means of production reunite—combining not organically, however, but perversely, as the playthings of a capitalist.

The proletarian finds her or himself abjectly dependent on the capitalist, for 'employment', for 'a chance to make a living', for access to means of production. Though the proletarian does all productive labour, the capitalist alone controls production—simply by owning the means of production, which allows him to buy and thus own labour-power as well.

13. A HISTORY LESSON

The historical expropriation of the direct producer took place originally in England, in the 15th, 16th and 17th centuries, and, later, throughout Europe and most of the world. In some places, this process is still going on, as producers the planet over become wage-earners.

Let's review the start of this process in England, that majestic isle, land of light and harmony where capital and the proletariat were born. It is a tale told in blood and fire ...

SHERWOOD FOREST *

GO AND CAPTURE ROBIN HOOD AND BRING HIM TO JUSTICE — AAAAAARGHH!!!

THWOK!!

* HOME OF ROBIN HOOD. PIONEER TRADE UNION ORGANISER AND PHILANTHROPIST.

Many moralists and politicians tell an edifying story designed to enlighten us about the happy origins of wealth and poverty. 'Long, long ago,' they say, 'there were two sorts of people: one, the diligent, intelligent, and above all frugal elite; the other, lazy rascals, spending their wealth, and more, in riotous living. Thus it came to pass that the latter sort finally had nothing to sell except their own skins. And from this original sin dates the poverty of the great majority (who, despite all their labour, have up to now nothing to sell but themselves), and the wealth of the few (that increases constantly, although they long ago ceased to work).'

In real history, conquest, enslavement, robbery and murder play the greatest part. Not only the working class, but poverty, welfare, colonialism and all the rest are the result not of frail 'human nature', but of an epic assault on the common people by bosses and aristocrats of every type.

Exploitation is nothing new. By "exploitation" we refer to the control of *surplus labour* by an oppressor class.

In slave society, the class of exploiters ruled coercively. The same was true when serfs were bound to the land and forbidden to move.

BRITAIN 1480   BRITAIN 1980s

But in capitalist society, the 'whip of hunger' keeps workers in line. Armed might is still used -- when strikes and protests grow unruly -- but only as a last resort. In quieter times, the sheer pressure of need -- for jobs, for wages -- keeps workers from resisting the extraction of surplus from their labour.

Why is **your** labor **my** surplus?

QUIET EXAM IN PROGRESS

Another new departure in capitalist society is that *surplus labour* becomes surplus ***abstract*** labor -- that is, what Marx called *surplus **value**.*

But what, exactly, is surplus labour?

Above and beyond labour necessary for survival—*necessary* labour—people may perform extra labour resulting in surplus product—*surplus labour.* The capacity for surplus labour is something that people acquire in stages. At first, in the most primitive societies, labour-power is relatively undeveloped—people are capable only of reproducing themselves, living at bare subsistence, picking fruits and berries, and so on. By arduous self-development, however, people master labour skills of greater power, like handicrafts and agriculture.

WHEN ADAM DELVED
AND EVE SPAN
WHO WAS THEN THE
GENTLEMAN

When labour-power finally develops to the point that surplus labour is possible, human existence is revolutionised.

INDEED, THE WHOLE DEVELOPMENT OF HUMAN SOCIETY BEGINS ON THE DAY WHEN THE LABOUR OF THE PRIMITIVE FAMILY CREATES MORE PRODUCTS THAN ARE NECESSARY FOR ITS MAINTENANCE. ON THE DAY WHEN THE FAMILY (SIC) DEVOTES A PORTION OF LABOUR NOT MERELY OF LIFES—

LAUNDROMAT

—NECESSITIES (MEANS OF SUBSISTENCE) BUT OF TOOLS AND MACHINES AS WELL (MEANS OF PROD-UCTION). SURPLUS PRODUCT BECOMES THE BASIS OF ALL SOCIAL, POLITICAL, AND INTELLECTUAL PROGRESS.

FREDERICK ENGELS.

Once the earliest communal cultures had waxed and waned, surplus labour fell under the sway of a sequence of exploiting classes. In slave societies, from Greek antiquity to the 'New World', slaveowners controlled surplus labour (and necessary labour, too). In feudal cultures, serfs performed surplus labour for landlords, working several days a week on the lord's land. In each case, the cream was skimmed from the top by an armed class of owners, the slave- owners and land-owners. 'Exploitation' is nothing else but the control exercised by oppressors over the surplus labour of the oppressed.

91

14. THE MAKING OF THE WORKING CLASS

In capitalist society, surplus labour is extracted from the proletariat in the form of surplus value. How this came to pass we can best understand by exploring the history of the expropriation of the producer. We must cast our eyes back to that time in English history when great masses of men, women and children were suddenly and forcibly torn from their means of production and hurled onto the labour-market as sellers of labour-power. The basis of this process was the expropriation of the peasant from the land.

AS A FREE PEASANT I'VE ONLY GOT A LITTLE PIECE OF LAND

- BUT I DON'T HAVE TO WORK FOR THE BARON ANYMORE.

THE BARON

-AND IT'S BETTER THAN WORKING FOR FORD

-OR WAITING FOR THE GRUNDRISSE.

ANYWAY. I CAN'T READ.

By the end of the 14th century, English serfdom had practically disappeared. The immense majority of the population consisted of free peasants. In contrast to earlier times, these peasants did relatively little work for the nobles, working instead on land commonly or privately owned. Though gigantic baronies were strewn about, small peasant properties were much more common.

The violent expropriation of these small properties and proprietors occurred in several phases. Thus was formed a propertyless proletariat. The opening shot in the campaign was fired by the monarchy. In a bold move to strengthen the king against the nobles, the royal power took action to dissolve the bands of retainers surrounding the various luminaries of the nobility.

YOU'RE AIDES DE CAMP—

SO DE-CAMP!

These *aides de camp* thus became the first to be hurled in appreciable numbers onto the early labour-market.

In defiant opposition, the great feudal lords created an incomparably larger proletariat, undertaking the forcible seizure of peasant land-holdings in a ruthless effort to magnify aristocratic power.

WE CALL IT 'FLEECING THE PEASANTRY,' OF COURSE!

The direct impulse for this process of expropriation was provided by the rapid expansion of wool manufacture in Flanders, and the corresponding rise in wool prices. Seeking money, that emerging power of powers, the nobility decided to convert farm lands into sheepwalks.

To do this, they concentrated all their military might on the peasantry in a vast, brutal, ultimately successful effort to uproot it, pillaging and razing countless villages in the process.

An Act from the time of Henry VIII speaks of the resulting transfer of control over the means of production, 'whereby many farms and large flocks of sheep became concentrated in the hands of a few men; whereby marvellous numbers of people have been deprived of the means wherewith to maintain themselves and their families.'

Henry's minister, Thomas More, speaks in Utopia of the curious land where

SHEEP SWALLOW DOWN THE VERY MEN THEMSELVES.

As Francis Bacon declared,

THIS BRED A DECAY OF PEOPLE, TOWNS, CHURCHES AND THE LIKE.

Once owners of several acres, the peasants now were virtually landless. To this day, the typical worker is lucky to own even a small garden.

The expropriation process received two new and terrible impulses during the 16th century: the theft, on a colossal scale, of Catholic Church lands (during the Protestant Reformation) and of State lands (during the 'Glorious Revolution' of 1688).

The overall result was that by methods of ruthless terrorism the lands of England were converted from community property and small holdings into a set of gigantic private business ventures. Meanwhile the numb of uprooted, propertyless, and rightless ex-peasants swelled beyond measure.

Where did these peasants go?

PAUPERS ARE
EVERYWHERE,
AND EVERYWHERE
SUBJECTED

Thus spoke Queen Elizabeth
after a journey through England.
Soon after, it proved necessary
to recognise pauperism
officially by the introduction
of the poor-rate.

But the powers-that-be did not generally
treat the refugee peasantry with anything
like kindness. Just the reverse. Incredible
new violence was visited upon these already
terrorised people, to transform them into a
passive, docile working class, to discipline
them to the regime of industry, to break
them of their rebellious spirit.

Far from all of the uprooted labourers
created by the expropriation of the
peasantry could be employed by nascent
industry. Abruptly dragged from their
accustomed life, with few opportunities for
wage-work, these unfortunates were turned
in huge numbers into beggars, robbers, and
vagabonds.

97

The State promptly showed its great and tender regard for the newly impoverished by enacting Draconian laws treating beggars and vagabonds as 'voluntary criminals.

- During the reign of Henry VIII, in 1530, vagabonds were condemned to whipping for a first offence, loss of an ear for a second, and execution for a third—with no help offered in finding work.

- During the reign of Edward VI, in 1547, anyone refusing to work—at what? with what means of production?—was condemned as a slave.

- During the reign of Elizabeth, in 1572, unlicensed beggars 14 or older were severely flogged and branded. A second offence brought death.

FRIENDS, ROMANS, VAGABONDS, LEND ME YOUR EARS!

HOPE THEY DON'T FIND OUT I'VE NEVER DONE A STROKE OF WORK IN MY ENTIRE LIFE!

'Thus were the farming folk of England expropriated, chased from their homes, turned into vagabonds, and then whipped, branded, and tortured by grotesquely terroristic laws into accepting the discipline necessary for the system of wage labour.'

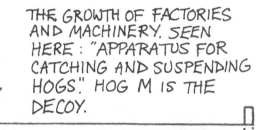

THE GROWTH OF FACTORIES AND MACHINERY. SEEN HERE: "APPARATUS FOR CATCHING AND SUSPENDING HOGS." HOG M IS THE DECOY.

With this background, money was at long last free to function as capital, buying great quantities of labour-power to carry on manufacture and, later, industrial production. Spindles, looms, and other means of production—once dispersed through the countryside—were now gathered together in primitive factories. Trade penetrated everywhere, powered by the incipient 'industrial revolution'. The combination of concentrated means of production and hired labour-power proved tremendously dynamic.

HOW COME M ALWAYS GETS THE GOOD JOBS?

'The discovery of gold and silver in America, the elimination, enslavement, and entombment in mines of the original American population, the beginnings of the conquest and plunder of India, and the conversion of Africa into a preserve for the commercial hunting of Black skins–these are the idyllic proceedings that characterized the dawn of capitalist production.'

GEOFF PERKS

JOHN BULL SAILED AROUND THE WORLD
TO LOOK FOR LAND TO SEIZE –
HE STOLE SOME ISLANDS IN THE WEST
AND CALLED THEM HIS WEST INDIES

At first, capital could absorb a mere fraction of the surplus population driven from the land, leaving beggars and vagbonds unemployed in droves. But, once underway, capitalist production gathered momentum. As decades and centuries passed, the immense majority of the English population became proletarians. The same happened elsewhere, too.

The terroristic methods and harsh laws by which the landless population had initially been introduced to labour discipline became decreasingly necessary as capitalist production stabilised, becoming the 'normal' form of production.

> 'Now, the silent compulsion of economic relations sets the seal on the domination of the capitalist over the worker. Direct extra-economic force is still of course used, but only in exceptional cases. In the ordinary run of things, workers can safely be left to the gentle mercy of production relations–to fears of joblessness, to hunger and need...'

Because they possess no means of production, workers have no option but to 'freely' sell their labour-power. It is in this way that the proletariat becomes the principal actor on the economic stage.

'SOME EXHIBITS WHICH WILL NOT BE ON SHOW AT THE GREAT EXHIBITION'. PUNCH, 1851.

Proletarians differ from openly unfree labourers like slaves and serfs in two ways. Unlike slaves, they are 'free' to sell their labour-power; unlike serfs, they are 'free' of land and other means of production. *This is the dual basis of the vaunted 'freedom' of bourgeois society.*

FREEDOM TO STARVE?

Workers, as Jeremy Benthan rejoiced, enjoy 'freedom,' 'equality' and the 'right' to property.

THAT'S EVERYBODY'S RIGHT, MY DEAR!

FREEDOM, because both buyer and seller are free to contract with others.

EQUALITY, because buyers and sellers interact as simple commodity owners, exchanging equivalent for equivalent.

PROPERTY, because buyers and sellers live only by exchanging what they own.

But when we leave the sphere of exchange—when we enter the hidden abode of *production,* on whose threshold hangs the notice, 'No admittance expect on business'—a certain change takes place in the manner of our leading characters.

The money-owner now strides forward as a capitalist; the possessor of labour-power follows as his worker. The one smirks self-importantly and is intent on business; the other is deferential and fearful. We are now speaking about the *alienation of labour*—the subordination of the worker to an alien power. As the direct outcome of the sale of labour-power, the subordination of the worker is an intrinsic feature of labour-power's status as a commodity. Comprising a false freedom—the 'freedom' to enter a subservient role—labour's alienation is the vital prerequisite for its exploitation.

The worker's freedom is a curious matter. It should be evident, on balance, that the worker, as a participant in commodity exchange, is free to do just one thing: sell time and energy for wages. Different bosses and different jobs are available but workers can avoid bosses and jobs only if they don't care about 'making a living'. Everyone knows that there are just two kinds of workers: employed and unemployed.

With the sale of labour-power, working people lose all control over what they do. What is produced and how—the purposes and methods of labour—are questions only the capitalist many answer. And the *result* of labour—the product itself—unquestionably belongs not to the producer but to the capitalist.

An alien will, concerned not about the worker but about profit, decides what the worker does. The motives of working people are entirely discounted in production, trampled by the profit-motive.

Moneybags sternly warns the worker:

JUST DO WHAT YOU'RE TOLD! THAT'S WHAT YOU'RE HERE FOR — YOU'RE NOT PAID TO THINK! WHAT YOU DO ON YOUR OWN TIME IS YOUR OWN AFFAIR, BUT HERE YOU DO WHAT I SAY. WHAT YOU PRODUCE IS NONE OF YOUR BUSINESS. IF YOU DON'T LIKE MAKING NERVE GAS, OR NEUTRON BOMBS OR DEFECTIVE CARS OR ADULTERATED FOODS, YOU CAN LOOK FOR WORK ELSEWHERE. DO I MAKE MYSELF CLEAR?

Workers are never allowed any say about what to produce or why.

'Investment decisions' -- *how* and *why* to employ labour-power and means of production, say, whether to make nuclear weapons or candy -- are the sole prerogative of capital.

LEAVE
YOUR
BRAIN
IN THE
RACK

By selling labour-power—a matter of 'free choice' in name only—the worker surrenders control over labour. In this way labour, the *use* of labour-power, is *alienated,* just as the use of commodities is alienated in general. The difference is that labour, once sold, can never be recovered.

Bread, though its usefulness is repressed while it awaits sale, can at least be eaten when it does sell. The use of labour-power, by contrast, is most fully alienated *after* its sale.

Though working people may resist the tyranny of the capitalist in various way, this is done at personal risk. Workers can be fired. The capitalist can refuse to continue buying labour-power. At this point, the worker is severed both from *means of production* and *means of subsistence.* Though resistance, to be sure, is possible and necessary it doesn't alter the basic fact that being a worker means being dependen on the capitalist.

And Moneybags has the law on his side. After all, he buys your labour-power, doesn't he? So it's his—to use as he likes. If you object, just ask the police—or the courts. You'll learn quickly enough that the use of labour-power belongs to its rightful, legal owner—Moneybags.

POLICE FIRE ON STRIKERS: U.S. 1932

15. SURPLUS VALUE

ACCUMULATE!
ACCUMULATE!
THAT IS
MOSES AND
THE PROPHETS
TO THE
CAPITALIST!

Alienation of labour is the fundamental prerequisite for its exploitation. Sold to be used, labour-power must be *alienated* to be *exploited.* It then becomes the source of surplus value.

Overcharging for commodities does *not* create surplus value; exploiting the working class *does*.

How so?

People have had the capacity to perform surplus labour for millennia, ever since the first revolution in agriculture. In contemporary, capitalist society, the primary result of surplus labour is *surplus value*. Remember M-C-M′? Capital seeks to expand—to multiply—to embody more abstract labour after investment than before.

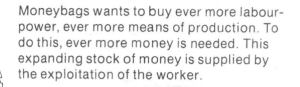

Moneybags wants to buy ever more labour-power, ever more means of production. To do this, ever more money is needed. This expanding stock of money is supplied by the exploitation of the worker.

THOUGH MARX HAD MANY WORTHY ANTECEDENTS - PETTY, BOISGUILLEBERT, FRANKLIN, GALIANI, STEUART, QUESNAY, RICARDO - IT WAS MARX'S INSIGHT THAT LED TO THE EXPLANATION OF SURPLUS VALUE. WHAT MARX DISCOVERED IS THAT THE VALUE OF LABOUR-POWER MAY BE LESS THAN THE VALUE OF THE LABOUR PRODUCT. THIS IS THE SECRET OF SURPLUS VALUE, AT LAST REVEALED.

109

What is the value of a commodity? Just this: the average, socially required labour-time necessary to make it. Since labour-power in capitalist society is also a commodity, it too, has a value. This is the average labour-time required to 'produce' the worker; to keep the worker alive and productive ... just what it costs to replenish the worker's energy, so that *tomorrow's* labour-power will be roughly the same as *today's*.

Historically, the work of reproducing labour-power has been reserved for women, as wives and mothers...

The signal fact is that workers are capable of producing commodities more valuable than labour-power itself.

8 HOURS FOR WORK • 8 HOURS FOR OUR OWN INSTRUCTION AND 8 HOURS FOR REPOSE • WE REQUIRE 8 HOURS FOR WORK •

The value of the labour product may exceed the value of labour-power—that is, the average labour-time socially required to keep a worker going may be less than the average, socially required labour-time the worker expends making commodities. Paying the worker for the value of his or her labour-power ordinarily requires less money than the capitalist gets in return for the product the worker produces.

111

Take any worker, at random. If $50 is the cost of supplying the worker with means of subsistence, a capitalist is foolhardy to pay this unless the worker's product (say, bread) turns out to be worth *more* than $50. Otherwise, the capitalist will go out of business. But if the worker does produce commodities worth more than the initial investment, all is well. The investment 'works': money is 'made'.

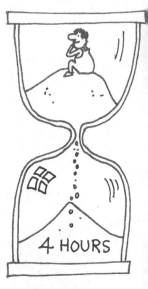

TIME IT TAKES FOR THE WORKER TO PROVIDE FOR HIMSELF.

If it happens that the worker produces commodities equal in value to the worker's labour-power in just *part* of a workday—say, in 4 hours—there is nothing to prevent the capitalist from employing the worker for *more* than 4 hours—say, 8 hours. When this does, in fact, happen (as it regularly does!), *surplus value* is the result.

TIME IT TAKES WHEN SURPLUS LABOUR IS ADDED ON.

The 4 hours necessary to produce commodities as valuable as the worker's labour-power we call (surprise!)— NECESSARY LABOUR. The *extra* time spent producing commodities we call SURPLUS LABOUR. Assuming that the worker spends roughly the average labour-time socially required to produce whatever is produced, this labour counts as so much abstract, socially equal labour-value. The surplus accumulated is surplus abstract labour—*surplus value*.

112

IF THE WORKER'S LABOUR IS SUB-AVERAGE, IT MAY STILL PRODUCE SURPLUS VALUE—BUT LESS. IT COUNTS AS LESS ABSTRACT LABOUR THAN IT WOULD HAVE IF IT HAD BEEN AT LEAST AVERAGE. FOR EXAMPLE: 8 HOURS OF LESS-THAN AVERAGE LABOUR MIGHT RESULT IN THE PRODUCTION OF COMMODITIES NORMALLY REQUIRING ONLY 6 HOURS TO PRODUCE. IT WOULD THUS COUNT AS ONLY 6 HOURS OF ABSTRACT LABOUR —BUT IF NECESSARY LABOUR REQUIRES ONLY 4 LABOUR HOURS THERE IS STILL A SURPLUS OF TWO. THIS IS ONLY HALF AS MUCH SURPLUS AS AVERAGE, BUT IT IS A SURPLUS. ON THE OTHER HAND, IF THE WORKER'S LABOUR IS SO SUB-AVERAGE THAT THE WORKER FAILS TO PRODUCE COMMODITIES OF ENOUGH VALUE TO COMPENSATE FOR PAYMENT OF WAGES THEN THE BOSS WILL GO BANKRUPT.

REASONABLE 'AVERAGE' MANAGEMENT

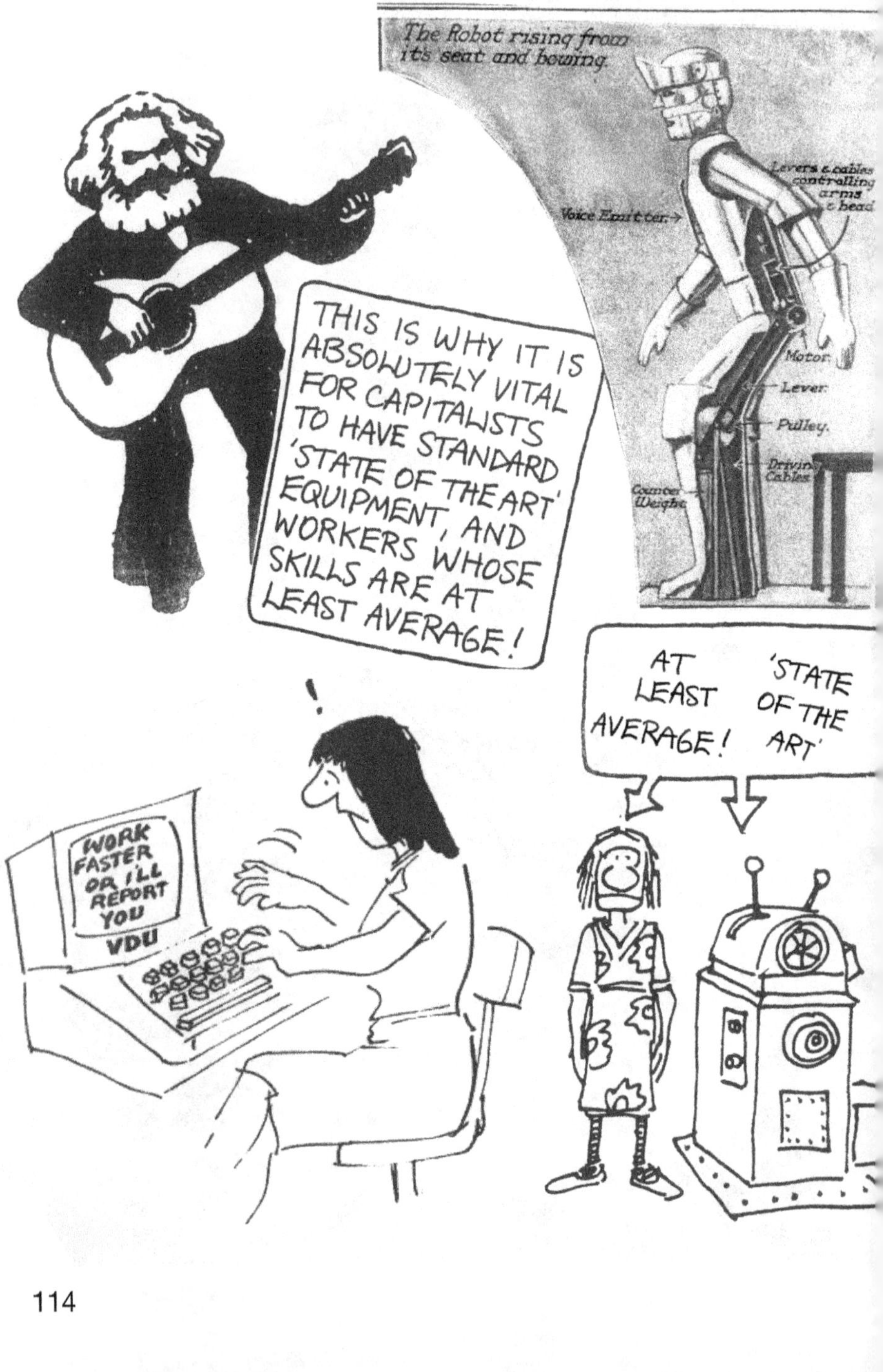
The Robot rising from it's seat and bowing.
Levers & cables controlling arms & head
Voice Emitter
Motor
Lever
Pulley
Driving Cables
THIS IS WHY IT IS ABSOLUTELY VITAL FOR CAPITALISTS TO HAVE STANDARD 'STATE OF THE ART' EQUIPMENT, AND WORKERS WHOSE SKILLS ARE AT LEAST AVERAGE!
!
AT LEAST AVERAGE!
'STATE OF THE ART'
WORK FASTER OR I'LL REPORT YOU
VDU

Moneybags buys two types of commodities to set the production process in motion -- our old friends labour-power and means of production!

Money thus functions as capital in two principal ways:

THE BOSS!

UNIT 798427...

1. Buying living human energy, and
2. Buying production equipment and resources (the product, in part, of the expenditure of previous living human energy)

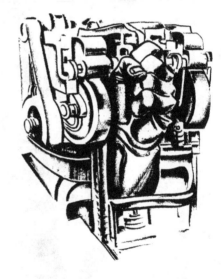

SURPLUS VALUE results from the use of just one of these two - labour-power.

The means of production also add **VALUE** to the product, but no more than they contain to begin with. No surplus, that is!

VARIABLE CAPITAL

This gives us our criterion for distinguishing different forms of capital. Since the value added to the commodity by labour-power *varies,* introducing the possibility of a surplus, we call the money spent for labour-power VARIABLE CAPITAL.

CONSTANT CAPITAL

Since the value contributed in production
by means of production does *not* vary, we
call money spent for means of production
CONSTANT CAPITAL.

THAT'S US!

VARIABLE CAPITAL

AND

CONSTANT CAPITAL

Why does constant capital generate no surplus value? Why, for example, does the contribution machinery makes to production not add more value than the value of the machinery itself?

Take any commodity at random, say, a watch. The value of the watch is the total quantity of average labour socially required to produce it. Right? This 'total quantity' of average labour includes, however, not *only* the useful labour directly spent making the watch—the labour involved in assembling the mechanism, connecting springs to wheels, setting the timer, inserting the glass, and so on—but also the labour embodied in the various tools and accessories necessary to make the watch.

In this case, we are speaking about various delicate instruments and machines, plus springs, wheels, glass and so on.

Moneybags buys these tools and accessory products so that a hired watchmaker can use them to make a watch.

In general, we assume that Moneybags buys this watch-making equipment for what it's worth—that is, an exchange of equivalents takes place; in which Moneybags pays as much for the equipment as the equipment is actually worth in terms of the abstract labour it contains.

If this happens, *no surplus value* will be created by the use of this equipment. Why not? Here's why:

| EXPLANATION |

Imagine, for a moment, that Moneybags purchases just enough watchmaking equipment (machinery and materials) to produce 100 watches. By the time these watches are completed, every machine will be used up and every accessory product will be used.

Assume further that the total value of this equipment is $1,000 —just what Moneybags pays for it. Now, if the total value of the watches is the quantity of average labour socially required to produce them, how much value will the watchmaking equipment add to these watches? *Just as much abstract labour as this equipment actually contains*—no more, and no less. Moneybags has paid for a specific sum of abstract labour— and this abstract labour then goes into the product Moneybags sponsors.

119

The total value of the watches is the sum of *two* elements:

the number of average labour
hours expended in producing
the equipment

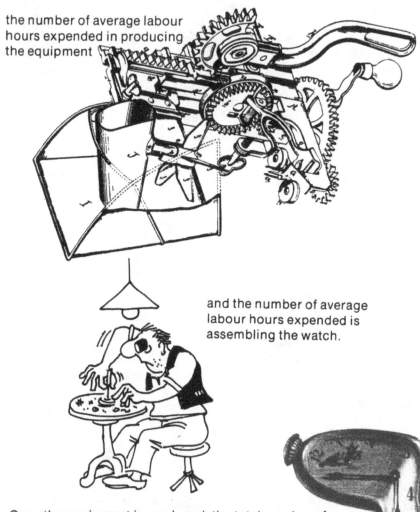

and the number of average
labour hours expended is
assembling the watch.

Once the equipment is produced, the total number of
hours it contains *will not change.* If the watches sell at their
value, say, $5,000, then we can be sure that the value added
by the watchmakers is $4,000. We already know how much
average labour went into the equipment—the equivalent of
$1,000. The value of this equipment *cannot rise* during the
production process; we can't pretend that more average
labour goes into this equipment than actually does.

120

NOW LET'S LOOK AT VALUE CREATION IN COMMODITY PRODUCTION ANOTHER WAY!

RAW MATERIALS
(Labour-Time: 3 hrs)

LABOUR
5 hrs

LABOUR-POWER
(Labour-Time: 0)

MEANS OF PRODUCTION
(machinery, semi-finished materials)
(Labour-Time: 5 hrs)

Surplus: 5 - 3 = 2 hrs.

Say that necessary labour-time = 3 hrs. It takes this long to produce items as valuable as the means of subsistence necessary to reproduce labour-power.

Set labour-power to work with no special equipment — just raw materials and skill — to produce means of production, i.e., the machinery and semi-finished materials necessary to make watches. Assume that zero socially required labour-time is embodied in the raw materials. If it now takes 5 hours of socially required labour to transform these genuinely 'raw' materials into watchmaking machinery and semi-finished materials —what is the value of this watchmaking equipment? Just 5 socially required labour-hours:

> *zero* labour hours to produce raw materials
> +
> *five* to transform raw materials into equipment.

since 3 labour-hours are socially required to reproduce power, surplus labour here = 2 hours: the difference between the time socially required for watchmaking equipment (5 average hours) and the time required for labour-power (3 average labour-hours).

121

—AND GOING ON WE FIND:

**MEANS OF
PRODUCTION**
(Labour-Time:
5 hrs)

LABOUR
12 hrs

**COMMODITIES
(WATCHES)**
(Labour-Time:
17 hrs)

LABOUR-POWER
(Labour-Time:
3 hrs)

Surplus:
12 - 3 = 9 hrs

If it requires *5 hours* to produce watch-making equipment, and then *12 hours* to use up this equipment making watches, what quantity of total, socially required labour-time goes into these watches?

That's simple arithmetic: 5 + 12 = 17. Exactly 17 labour-hours are required to produce and use means of production for the production of watches for sale. All socially required labour-power is now present and accounted for. But how much surplus value is generated in this watchmaking process?

If necessary labour-time — the value of labour-power – equals 3 average labour-hours, and total labour-time - the value of the labour product – equals 12 average hours, the difference is surplus value: 12 - 3 + 9. Assuming that the watchmakers receive the equivalent (in wages) of 3 labour-hours, Moneybags thus accrues the equivalent (in money) of 9 labour-hours. That's surplus value.

Do the means of production add to this surplus value? No! The total value of the product unquestionably includes the labour-time socially required to produce means of production. As we've seen, the total value of the watches = 17 labour-hours: 12 using means of production plus 5 making means of production. But surplus value results only from the difference between the value created and the value presupposed — and only labour-power creates more value than it presupposes. Means of production, used up in production, add just the value they contain; in this case, 5 labour-hours.

To be sure, production of means of production may generate surplus value. (Indeed, as we saw earlier, if it takes 5 labour-hours to produce watchmaking equipment but only 3 labour-hours to reproduce labour-power, surplus value does accrue.) But again: this surplus value is created by the exercise of labour-power, which thus shows itself capable of creating products more valuable than itself (by a ratio of 5:3, in this case).

16. THE RATE OF SURPLUS VALUE

In M-C-M′, the basic change is from M to M^1. We can now show this by two new equations:

1. Capital = constant capital + variable capital, or Capital = c + v.
2. Capital′ = constant capital + variable capital + *surplus value*, or Capital′ = c + v + s.

c = constant capital
v = variable capital
s = surplus value

I TRY TO KEEP THIS **DOWN**—

The difference between Capital—Capital′ (or between M-M′, if this is how we choose to depict it) is *surplus value,* s.

Since v is the source of s, it makes sense to compare s and v. Surplus value/variable capital is the *rate of surplus value.* When v = 5 and s = 5, s/v = 1—in other words, this represents an exactly 100% rate of surplus value.

THE RATE OF PROFIT

—AND I TRY TO KEEP THIS **UP**!

The RATE OF PROFIT is the ratio between s and total investment, both constant *and* variable capital—that is, s/v+c, or s/Capital.

Whenever c is greater than zero, the rate of profit is less than the rate of surplus value. **This is very important.** Why? Because it helps to explain why there is a tendency for the rate of profit to *fall;* why capitalism tends to profit-crunches; why, in a word, economic crisis is such a basic part of life in capitalist society.

When *c rises* there tend to be *crises!*

123

The ratio of constant to variable capital we call the ORGANIC COMPOSITION OF CAPITAL. When c rises relative to v, we say that the organic composition of capital *rises*. In other words, the more means of production are employed relative to labour-power, the higher is the organic composition of capital.

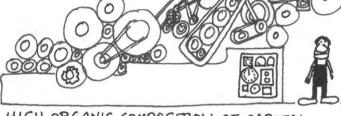

HIGH ORGANIC COMPOSITION OF CAPITAL.

LOW ORGANIC COMPOSITION OF CAPITAL.

As everyone knows, capital production tends to rely ever more on increasingly powerful means of production. Every day, high technology gets higher—more powerful machines enter production, and productivity soars. From simple hand tools-spindles, looms, hammers, anvils-production advances to nuclear power plants, automated factories, advanced computer systems, and much, much more.

Historically, the most important reason for the rapid growth of capitalist-owned means of production is *competition*. When Moneybags decides to buy labour-power and means of production to produce watches, he embarks on a risky venture. There are other firms making watches, and a less-than-infinite market. Who can sell watches? How many can be sold? For what price?

If Moneybags is fortunate, he, rather than his competitors, will get a large share of the market. To do this, though, Moneybags needs to sell his products as cheaply as possible. Unless he is willing to sell products for less than they are worth (which sometimes happens, but as an exception, not the rule), this means that he must cut the average labour-time socially required for the production of watches. If it originally requires 20 hours of average labour-time to make a watch, Moneybags must find some way to produce a watch in *less* than 20 hours.

125

When he does, he can then charge less for his product with no loss in surplus value, and win a higher percentage of the market. If his competitor, Cashbox, finds a way to cut prices by cutting labour-time, Moneybags must follow suit—or go out of business when Cashbox 'corners the market'.

To make a long, unlovely story shorter and sweeter, the point is that competition forces capital to use ever less labour-time per commodity. First, Moneybags cuts the time required to produce a watch from 20 hours to 18. Then Cashbox retaliates by cutting it still further. And so it goes, like a tug of war. Cutting prices, as we will see, is a way to cut throats—to eliminate competitors.

HOW IS AVERAGE LABOUR-TIME REDUCED?

EASY, FRED! BY INCREASING THE POWER OF THE MEANS OF PRODUCTION! THE TIME SPENT PRODUCING A TOOL IS GENERALLY FAR LESS THAN THE TIME THE TOOL SAVES. OTHERWISE, WHY PRODUCE IT?

EVEN IF THE INSTRUMENT ITSELF REQUIRES PRODIGIOUS TIME AND ENERGY—SAY AN OIL REFINERY—THE TIME AND ENERGY IT SAVES IS EVEN MORE PRODIGIOUS. IF IT TAKES 70 EXTRA HOURS TO MAKE AN ELECTRIC TYPEWRITER SELF-CORRECTING, THE TIME THIS SAVES LATER IN CORRECTING ERRORS ON TENS OF THOUSANDS OF PAGES WILL BE ENORMOUS!

(YOUR AUTHOR) NO KIDDING!

And this is even more true for more powerful instruments.

127

The golden rule of competitive profit-making is to produce *more* for *less*—to cut costs by cutting the average labour-time required for production. How? By increasing the power of the means of production.

IN STALIN'S RUSSIA IN THE 1930'S ALEXEI STAKHANOV, A MINER, (RT) VASTLY EXCEEDED NORMAL OUTPUT. STALIN SENT HIM ROUND THE COUNTRY TO PREACH 'STAKHANOVISM'.

BUT THE OTHER WORKERS SAID:

IF STAKHANOV IS SO KEEN—

—LET **HIM** DO ALL THE WORK!

It's a simple rule—but one with earthshaking consequences. Productivity, revolutionised, rises steeply. The world fills with commodities, and the danger of economic crisis approaches.

What's the connection? Just this: *that s derives from v. Variable capital, not constant capital,* produces surplus value. If competition forces capital to employ an ever higher ratio of constant to variable capital—as it clearly does—then the rate of profit ($s/v+c$) tends to fall.

When more is spent on means of production relative to labour-power, the rate of profit tends to decline. Say, for example, that initially $c = 16$, $v = 8$, and $s = 8$ (so that a 100% rate of surplus value, s/v, obtains). If c rises with no corresponding rise in v and s, the rate of profit grows smaller (even though the rate of surplus value does not). Say c changes to c = *24. Then s/v+c changes from (8/8+16 = 1/3) to 8/8+24 = 1/4).*

From the standpoint of the capitalist, this is a big and appalling drop.

A RAILWAY MEETING : EMOTION OF THE SHAREHOLDERS AT THE ANNOUNCEMENT OF A DIVIDEND OF $2\frac{1}{2}$D.

Producing for exchange is risky—it's possible that the product will fail to sell, either as a result of competition or for other reasons.

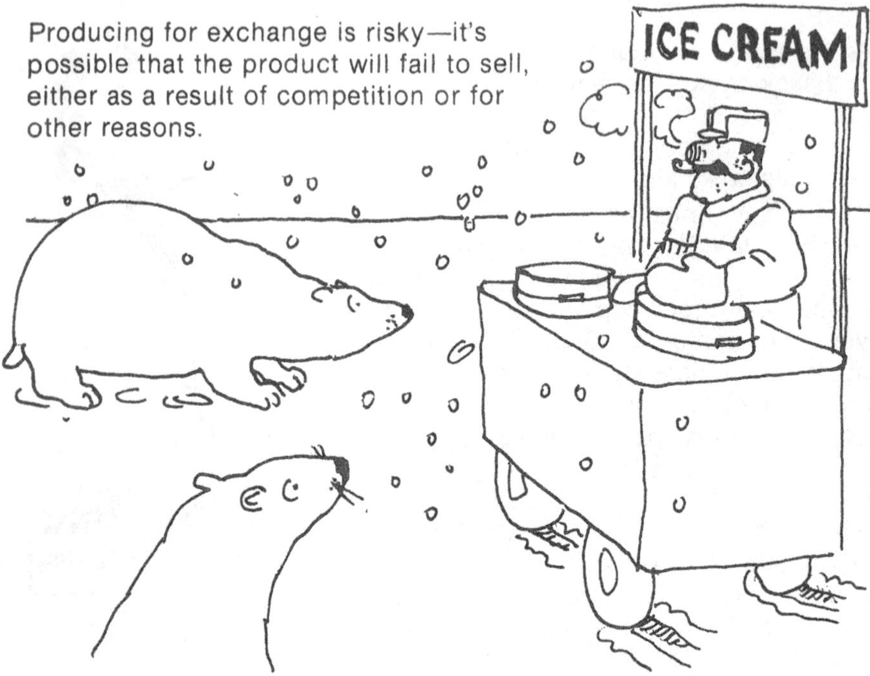
ICE CREAM

To make the gamble of investment worthwhile requires a certain minimum prospect of gain. If the rate of profit falls too low, investment ceases to be a wise use of money—the risk of loss is too great, the potential for gain is too slight.

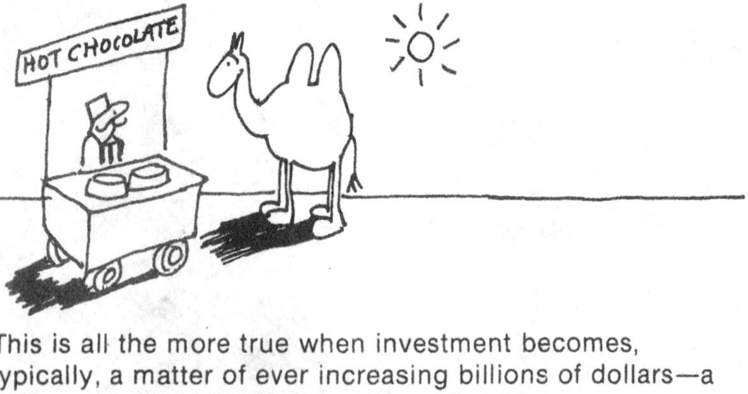
HOT CHOCOLATE

This is all the more true when investment becomes, typically, a matter of ever increasing billions of dollars—a tendency which parallels the tendency of the organic composition of capital to rise, and the tendency of the rate of profit to fall.

This is not just hypothetical. That the rate of profit has a tendency to fall is borne out by myriad facts of economic history. This tendency is not, however, *absolute.* There are *countertendencies* as well. But who can fail to notice the profit squeeze now stalking the world?

SPEAKING HISTORICALLY WE KNOW THAT 'C' RISES FASTER THAN 'V'. EVERY YEAR MORE MEANS OF PRODUCTION ARE EMPLOYED PER UNIT OF LABOUR-POWER. THOUGH THE TOTAL NUMBER OF WORKERS RISES TOO, THE WORLD OVER, THIS HAPPENS AT A SLOWER PACE THAN THE RATE AT WHICH THE TOTAL MASS OF MEANS OF PRODUCTION GROWS. IN GENERAL, AS A RESULT, S/V+C DECLINES OVER TIME. THE RATE OF PROFIT FALLS.

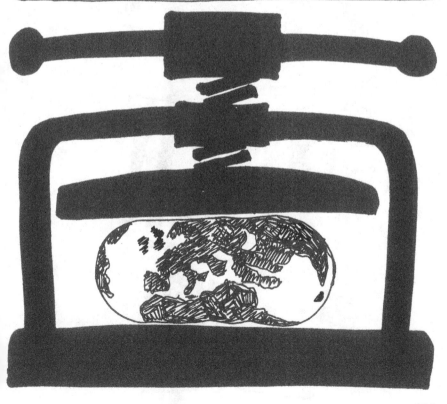

Previous profit squeezes have led to trade wars, often culminating in shooting wars. For competition leads not just to *cutthroat business*—Moneybags and Cashbox battling over price and markets—but to the *business of cutting throats*.

War is the ultimate means of securing economic advantage, letting your competitors suffer whatever losses must be incurred while you seize resources and markets directly without recourse to the genteel etiquette of exchange. For the victor, it is an excellent means of evading a fall in profits.

$$M - C - M$$

$$E = MC^2$$

WAR!

ALSO LATE FOOTBALL RESULTS

Some of the countertendencies to the tendency for the rate of profit to fall are vastly important, not only as such, but in their own right. These countertendencies revolve around v (variable capital) and s (surplus value). If c rises, what can maintain or improve the rate of profit? A comparable increase in s or a decrease in v? Let's consider these in turn.

OH, MARY – DIDN'T I TELL YOU –

– WE'VE INCREASED THE LENGTH OF THE WORKING DAY!

If necessary labour is still 4 hours, and if the number of workers stays constant, then extra surplus value can be extracted by adding extra hours to the working day. A working day of 8 hours will yield 4 hours. of unpaid surplus labour-time— but a working day of 10 hours will yield 6, and a working day of 12 hours will *double* the original surplus value. With no change in v—neither the value of the labour-power nor the total number of workers changes—s *rises*.

This we call the extraction of ABSOLUTE SURPLUS VALUE.

By compelling the worker to work longer hours, Moneybags forces an absolute increase in surplus value. This is pure, unbridled joy for the capitalist, the pleasure of getting something for nothing. For the worker, the compulsory performance of absolutely more surplus labour is something else entirely--a journey through purgatory, into the hell of overwork.

Is it accidental that the antagonistic relations between capital and labour so constantly revolve around the length of the working day? No! Starting with legal enactments in the 14th century, capital has fought long and hard to keep workers *at work* as much as possible.

In the brutal glory days of early English capitalism -- when capital was organised but labour wasn't -- horror stories abounded.

Countless thousands of children between 7 and 12 were worked to death, forced to work from before sunrise until midnight or later.

Capital's voracious appetite for labour brought death to myriad workers, young and old.

Most of the time, there were no workplace regulations at all --
just the ceaseless torment of hot, dangerous work in lightless,
chokingly dirty factories and mines.

Children, women, and men suffered through brutish and nasty lives
shortened by overwork. Penniless even when employed, workers in
these 'dark satanic mills' (so-called by the poet William Blake) were
crippled and maimed in innumerable ways. Domestic life was totally
disrupted, with entire families chained to machines...

The only power serving to limit capital's effort to turn every waking hour into a working hour was the working class itself. By stubborn struggle against a powerful foe -- a foe defended by the armed might of the state -- workers organised to pare the working day to human proportions. Success smiled upon many of these efforts. Moneybags yielded grudgingly, forced to swallow gall and wormwood in the form of an abbreviated workday, scaled back, at first, to 10 hours, and later to eight.

Capital despises this misfortune, resisting the reduction of the workday with all its might -- seeking, even now, to undermine workers' gains by seeking out places where unorganised workers may be pressured into working 16 hour and 18 hour days.

8 HOURS FOR WORK · 8 HOURS FOR OUR OWN INSTRUCTION AND 8 HOURS FOR REPOSE · WE WI...

In many places, most notably where industry and a wage-earning class are recent developments, capital has the upper hand.

Consider Bangladesh, Vietnam, Angola...

So the battle over *absolute surplus value* continues. S rises and falls at different times and in different parts of the world as the balance of power between capital and labour see-saws back and forth. Here labour forces absolute surplus value down— there capital forces it up.

Meanwhile, there are other fronts in the battle over surplus value. Say, for example, that workers are forced to work *faster*. If the value of labour-power remains unchanged, then it now requires fewer labour hours to produce commodities equal in value to the value of labour-power.

Working faster, our harassed worker produces in three hours what formerly required 4 hours to produce. Where once 4 hours comprised necessary labour-time, now 3 hours does so. Even without lengthening the working day, capital can thus extract extra surplus value. An extra hour of surplus labour is extracted—and *every* hour of surplus labour is now equal to 4/3 of one labour hour *before* the work was speeded up. If we assume that the earlier labour was socially average, the present, faster labour is *above average* in intensity, resolving itself into *more* hours of *average* labour than before.

Six thousand cars a day! By God, Elmer,
where do you get all your energy?

Or suppose that the *value of labour-power* falls. This occurs, willy nilly, whenever the average labour-time socially required to produce the means of subsistence falls. By means of rising productivity in the food industry, the construction trades, and related industries, foodstuffs and other basic subsistence necessitities may be sold at cheaper prices.

When this happens, the value of labour-power—roughly, the cost of reproducing labour-power through the purchase of basic necessities—also falls. The result is that *fewer* hours of labour are now required to produce commodities as valuable as labour-power—since the value of labour-power has *fallen.*

By reducing that part of the workday devoted to necessary labour in either of these two ways—by speedup, or by cutting the value of labour-power—capital extracts what we call RELATIVE SURPLUS VALUE. Without *absolutely* lengthening the workday, capital nevertheless succeeds in expanding s by freeing *relatively* more of the workday for unpaid surplus labour.

Again, s rises—counteracting the tendency of the rate of profit to fall. And again, it is only the working class that can defend itself.

Speedup can be prevented from reaching a killing pace only by the action of workers organised for their own ends—as the telling lessons of sweatshop labour make clear. In countless places, Moneybags, Cashbox, and their bloodthirsty colleagues try to push labour faster, faster, and still faster—typically, by the ploy of speeding up the machines until the workers keel over. Or they turn to the ruse of 'scientific management,' bringing in 'efficiency experts' with stopwatches (à la Frederick Winslow Taylor) to reduce 'wasted motions' and thus generate higher productivity.

Or management psychology is used: 'What colour should we paint the factory, and what *muzak* should we play, to lull the workers into working harder?' Or direct force is employed, with the use of brutal foremen and supervisors.

Where labour is strong,
speed-up is kept in check.
But where labour remains
weak, capitalists speed workers
as fast as they can, as long as they can...

Until labour is strong everywhere, capital will scour the earth for unorganised workers who can be exploited more energetically than organised labour will allow.

HM - THAT VIBRATION COULD BE HARMFUL TO THE MACHINE !

Right now, as global labor grows steadily, capital has many options. Labour can be forced to provide more and still more surplus value, either absolutely (by elongating the workday) or relatively (by enhancing "productivity"). This significantly counteracts the tendency of the rate of profit to fall. Add to this that **v** can be lowered by layoffs, or by wage cuts, and we begin to glimpse the battery of options open to capital in its effort to avert the **crises** that threaten as **c rises.**

142

17. LABOUR-POWER AND CLASS STRUGGLE

Speaking of the value of labour-power raises several related questions. To begin with, how can we say how much labour-time is 'socially required' to reproduce labour-power?

It is clear that most working people live not at the level of bare subsistence required for simple biological survival, but at a level of subsistence defined *socially*. What workers need is not determined by nature alone, but by social custom. An historical, social, and moral element is present in the definition of the value of labour-power.

Vitally, therefore, the antagonism between capital and labour expresses itself in conflict over just how much workers require. When the working class is strong in particular regions or countries, workers can enforce a relatively higher standard of living—a relatively higher value of labour-power—than in places where they are weak.

This reveals several basic facts. On the one hand, we are reminded of the reality that value is not *natural, but social*—people *treat* some labour product as a commodity, *making* the labour going into the commodity 'abstract, socially standard.'

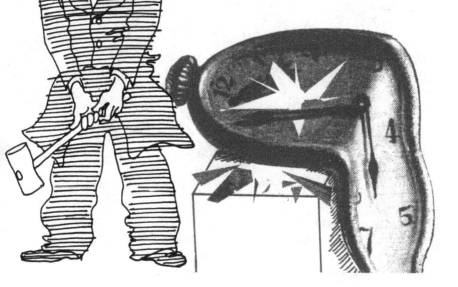

SINCE LABOUR IS ABSTRACT NOT MATERIALLY BUT AS A RESULT OF SOCIAL PRACTICE, WE CANNOT MEASURE ITS MAGNITUDE WITH A CLOCK. HOW MUCH 'ABSTRACT LABOUR-TIME' GOES INTO A COMMODITY IS, INDEED, BASED ON A CALCULATION OF REAL LABOUR-TIME, BUT AVERAGE LABOUR-TIME IS SOMETHING ABSTRACT

The social nature of value is never more
strikingly clear than in the case of the value
of labour-power. Though it is widely agreed
that workers should be paid 'a living wage' --
'enough to keep food on the table' -- 'enough
to keep the wolf away from the door' -- *what
constitutes a living wage is hotly contested.*
The idea is that people who work for a living
should not be denied the bare necessities.
But what counts as a 'necessity'?

What do workers *deserve?* What is a 'fair day's labor
worth? This is a matter of judgment -- and struggle!

For Moneybags, wages are a necessary evil -- which, if he can, he will cut to the bone.

The only way to prevent this is workers' self-organisation.

When Moneybags & Co. prevail, wages plummet. But when workers unite, they find new strength.

Wage increases are one natural consequence...

At any given moment, the level of wages reflects the
balance of power between capital and labour.

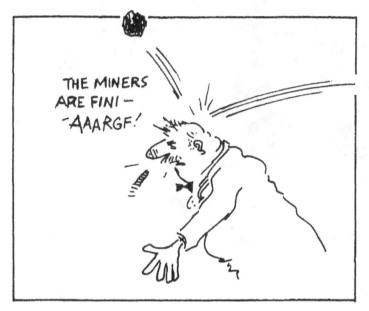

THE FIXATION OF ITS ACTUAL DEGREE
IS ONLY SETTLED BY THE CONTINUOUS
STRUGGLE BETWEEN CAPITAL AND LABOUR,
THE CAPITALIST CONSTANTLY TENDING
TO REDUCE WAGES TO THEIR PHYSICAL
MINIMUM WHILE WORKING PEOPLE
CONSTANTLY PRESS IN THE OPPOSITE DIRECTION.
THE QUESTION RESOLVES ITSELF INTO A
QUESTION OF THE RESPECTIVE POWERS
OF THE COMBATANTS.

When working people are powerful enough to put the fear of labour into capital, they push wages up. But capital has many resources. Sly as a fox, and no angel—with no mercy in his heart, and his heart in his wallet—a wondrous thing!—Moneybags relies on many strategems. Forced to pay high wages in one place, Moneybags will invest elsewhere to secure 'cheap labour,' that is, labour power requiring less socially average labour for its reproduction than the labour-power of better paid workers.

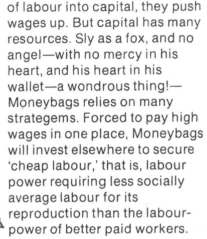

If workers in one part of the world accept a 'living standard' lower than that of workers elsewhere, the higher standard can be directly challenged—Moneybags will simply hire cheap rather than expensive labour-power, forcing better paid workers to moderate their wage demands (if they desire to keep their jobs).

This is merely one example of competition between workers—competition between sellers of labour-power, who, like all sellers, must keep their prices 'competitive' if they hope to sell.

Sometimes, capitalists will accede to relatively high wage payment: to encourage worker loyalty when profits are high, to divide higher from lower paid workers, or to hire workers with special skills. But never is this done altruistically. *Moneybags wants surplus value*, and surplus value is the difference between the value of labour-power—represented by wages—and the value of the labour *product*—represented by price. All else being equal, the lower the wages, the higher the profits. Moneybags wants low wages!

Rivalry between workers is exploited to the fullest. In 1870, just as Marx began writing *Capital* Vol. 2, France and Prussia went to war. This was the first of the trio of fateful Franco-German wars that, within 75 years, were to lay waste to Europe. It was also, for Marx, a typical war of the capitalist era, pitting young workers of one nationality, the "flower of the working class," against young workers of other nationalities.

Such wars are fought on behalf of the rulers and the rich. But the victims, Marx said (workers in uniform and civilians who get caught in the crossfire) are asked to sacrifice in the name of national glory and honor. All too often, imbued with nationalist prejudices and fearful that foreign workers threaten their livelihoods, workers take up arms against each other.

The Franco-Prussian war of 1870 was, for Marx, the model of such a war. The truth of such wars, he said, was revealed when the Parisian workers revolted against their rulers and the war, declaring Paris to be a liberated commune. Hastily, the Prussian and French authorities put their hostilities on hold, marching to Paris *together* to suppress the Commune.

Capital, Marx said, has it both ways. In times of peace, when workers win higher wages, employers send jobs abroad. And in wartime, the rulers capitalize on the very rivalries they intensify in this way to send young workers abroad to suppress the revolts of the foreign poor.

So the question of what was later called 'imperialism' arises.
For many reasons, the capitalists of one nation find it attractive
to invest in other, typically poorer nations. Fresh markets,
investment opportunities, cheap labour-power and inexpensive
resources are available, to say nothing of coveted political and
military influence.

When access to these assets is threatened by the self-
organization of the poor and oppressed in these nations,
Moneybags recruits the poor and oppressed at home to repress
them. Serving as the pool from which soldiers are recruited,
young workers and the jobless are thus doubly central to capital
At the same time, fear and dislike of the foreign poor must be
nurtured. Though mainly emotional in origin and effects, these
feelings have roots, as well, in the *rivalry* between workers.

The workers of the great powers -- who are often relatively well paid, thanks to unionization -- prize their comparative affluence. They fear the devaluation of their labour-power that could result from the competition of poorer workers. Anxious to preserve their hard-won gains -- as well they should be! -- better-paid workers too often see workers elsewhere in a harsh light, showing more trust in their employers than in their fellow workers.

This allows Moneybags the best of both worlds -- to exploit workers at home and abroad, simultaneously enjoying the *support* of workers at home while reaping the *benefit* of paying low wages abroad. And more's the pity, since exploitation can only be effectively resisted by the *united* efforts of the exploited.

18. ABOLITION OF WAGE-LABOUR

So far, all our talk has been about *labour-power as a commodity*—bought and sold, turning into *alienated labour* when exercised under the thumb of a capitalist's alien, profit-oriented will. We have seen that the value of that remarkable commodity, labour-power, is an issue of permanent interest to capital and labour, as capitalists bend every effort to cheapen labour-power while workers try to increase its value.

BUT RARELY IS THE DEEPER QUESTION ASKED: WHY SHOULD LABOUR-POWER BE A COMMODITY AT ALL? WHY SHOULD CAPITALISTS CONTROL THE EXERCISE OF LABOUR-POWER, GIVING RISE TO ALIENATED LABOUR AND SURPLUS VALUE —

—WHEN WORKERS COULD RULE THEMSELVES, PRODUCING A MATERIAL SURPLUS TO MEET ACTUAL HUMAN NEEDS?

Nor is the ultimate answer to this question often grasped: That workers can seek not merely to enhance the price of their labour-power, but can, in fact, refuse to treat their labour-power *as a commodity.* The ability to work does *not* have to be valued in money; labour-power does not have to sell for wages. Rather, 'living labour-power' -- actual workers -- can unite for equal, democratic, nationless cooperative production.

This would be *socialism* in the true sense of the word -- ordinary working people in shared democratic control of production and social life, producing for use, not for sale and profit; cooperatively sharing, not competitively selling.

Shared freedom and power would be the hallmark of socialist society -- a society without bosses of any kind.

WORKING PEOPLE SHOULD NOT BE EXCLUSIVELY ABSORBED IN THE UNAVOIDABLE GUERRILLA FIGHTS INCESSANTLY SPRINGING UP FROM CAPITAL'S NEVER-CEASING EFFORTS TO CUT WAGES AND JOB SECURITY, ITS ATTACKS ON UNIONS, ETC. WORKERS SHOULD UNDERSTAND THAT, WITH ALL THE MISERIES IT IMPOSES, THE CAPITALIST SYSTEM ENGENDERS PRODUCTION SO POWERFUL THAT A NEW SOCIETY OF MATERIAL ABUNDANCE AND SOCIAL FREEDOM IS POSSIBLE. INSTEAD OF THE CONSERVATIVE MOTTO 'A FAIR DAY'S WAGE FOR A FAIR DAY'S WORK!', WORKERS SHOULD INSCRIBE ON THEIR BANNER THE REVOLUTIONARY WATCHWORD —

ABOLITION OF THE WAGES SYSTEM

THE 'LABOUR' MAY-DAY 1891

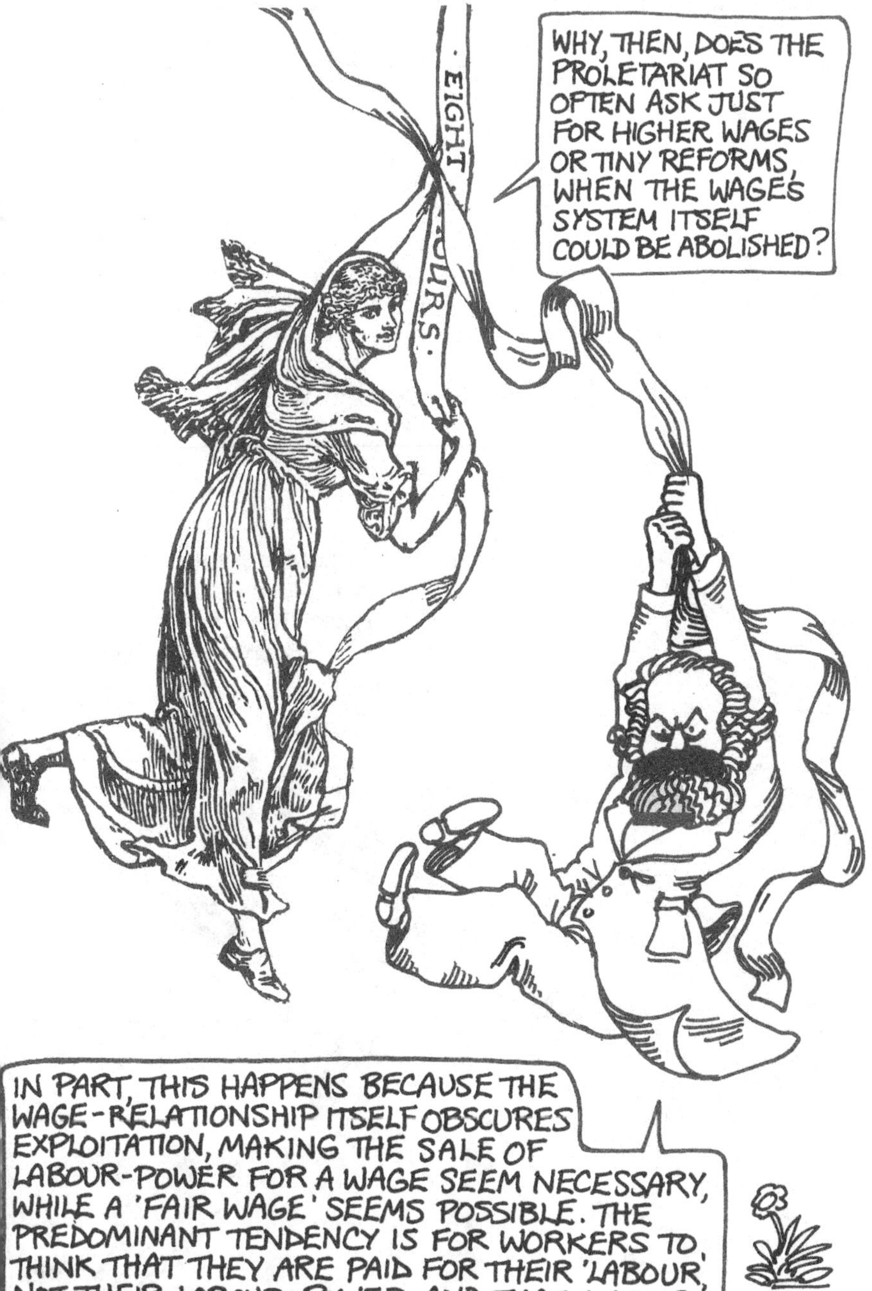

EIGHT HOURS.
WHY, THEN, DOES THE PROLETARIAT SO OFTEN ASK JUST FOR HIGHER WAGES OR TINY REFORMS, WHEN THE WAGES SYSTEM ITSELF COULD BE ABOLISHED?
IN PART, THIS HAPPENS BECAUSE THE WAGE-RELATIONSHIP ITSELF OBSCURES EXPLOITATION, MAKING THE SALE OF LABOUR-POWER FOR A WAGE SEEM NECESSARY, WHILE A 'FAIR WAGE' SEEMS POSSIBLE. THE PREDOMINANT TENDENCY IS FOR WORKERS TO THINK THAT THEY ARE PAID FOR THEIR 'LABOUR', NOT THEIR LABOUR-POWER, AND THAT A 'FAIR DAY'S WAGE' IS ALL THEY CAN HOPE FOR.

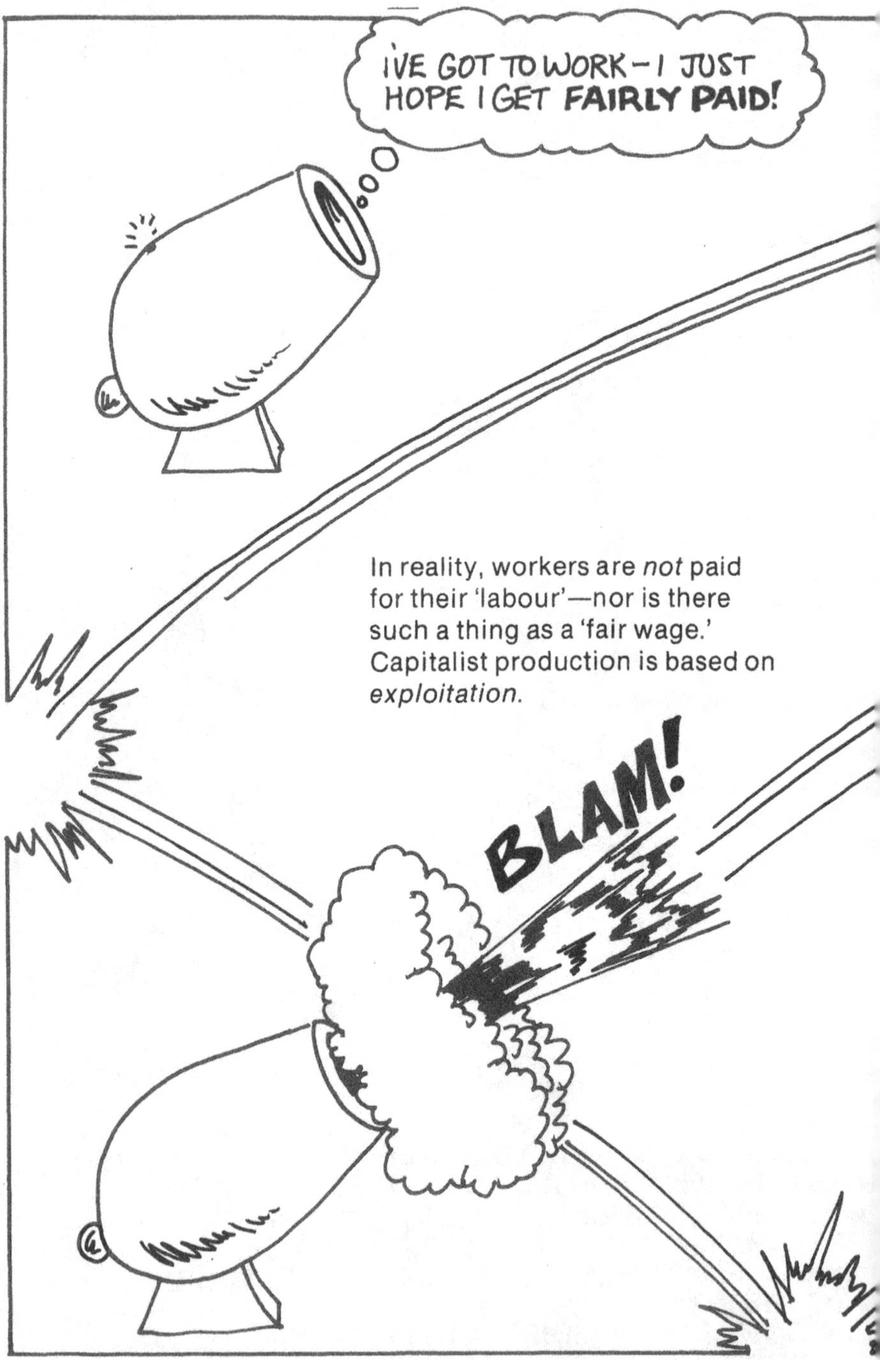
I'VE GOT TO WORK—I JUST HOPE I GET **FAIRLY PAID!**
In reality, workers are *not* paid for their 'labour'—nor is there such a thing as a 'fair wage.' Capitalist production is based on *exploitation.*
BLAM!

Once labour-power is sold, the capitalist uses it as he likes. Workers are paid not for their *own* labour, either useful or 'socially average,' but for the average labour-time required to *reproduce labour-power.*

This payment is equivalent in value only to part of the average labour performed by the worker—beyond this, there is *unpaid surplus labour.*

Workers seldom realise this. Instead, it is common to believe that working people are paid for *all* their labour—so that profits *do not* result from the exploitation of labour.

159

The wage-form thus extinguishes every trace of the division of the working day into necessary labour and surplus labour, into paid and unpaid labour. All labour appears as paid labour'.

FEUDAL LABOUR

Under the *corvée* system, in feudal times, it is different. There the labour of the serf for himself, and his compulsory labour for the lord of the land, are demarcated very clearly both in time and space.

SLAVE LABOUR

In slave labour, even the part of the working day in which the slave is only replacing the value of his own means of subsistence, in which he therefore actually works for himself alone, appears as labour for his master. *All* his labour appears as *unpaid* labour.

WAGE LABOUR

In wage-labour, on the contrary, even surplus labour, or unpaid labour, appears as paid.

The exchange between capital and labour seems just like the sale of any commodity. The sale itself seems preordained. After all, reasons the worker,

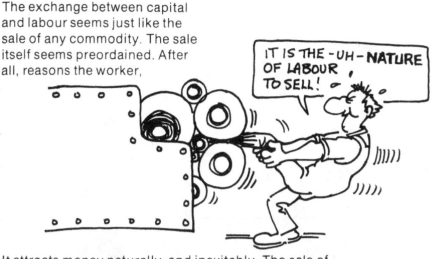

IT IS THE -UH- **NATURE** OF LABOUR, TO SELL!

It attracts money naturally, and inevitably. The sale of labour-power resulting in the alienation of labour appears to be a datum of nature, unalterable by human intervention. And what appears to sell is not labour-power, but labour.

Fetishism—the belief that labour-power's commodity status is an immutable fact of life—is thus coupled with a misperception of the commodity itself that disguises the reality of exploitation.

It's just a cigar!

Since workers are paid *after* they work, it seems that it is their *work,* not their *ability* to work, which is purchased. Moreover, working people imagine that it is natural for labour-power to sell. 'What else is possible?' This is *fetishism:* the perception that the commodity is intrinsically exchangeable.

161

Like all other commodities, 'labour' seems to have a certain natural exchange-value— a natural price. Hence the widespread faith in that phantom, 'a fair day's wage for a fair day's work.' The truth of the matter is that the unicorn is more common—or the dragon, the griffin, the leprechaun, the kind-hearted corporation and the honest politician.

NOW DO YOU BELIEVE IN A 'FAIR WAGE'?

But people don't usually realise this. Thinking that labour *must* sell as a commodity because this is its *nature*, workers hope for nothing more than a fair wage. In this way they mistake exploitation for nature, seeing no chance for real, unalienated freedom and power.

'All the notions of justice held by both the worker and the capitalist, all the mystifications of the capitalist mode of production, all capitalism's illusions about freedom, all the apologetic tricks of vulgar economics, have as their basis the appearance that wages are 'natural' and potentially 'fair.'

WHY DON'T YOU STOP READING THIS BOOK NOW AND SWITCH ON THE T.V.?

They are not, nor can they be. It is not 'natural' for workers to be divorced from the means of production. This, we have seen, is the result of an agonising historical process -- that of *expropriation.* Labour-power is sold to capital only because capital monopolizes the means of production. So-called 'free workers' -- who are free above all to alienate their labour for the privilege of exploitation -- are free only formally. They are free to *sell* their labour-power, but not to enjoy it and expend it for purposes of their own.

Without capital -- without business owners empowered by the possession of money to buy and control labour-power -- workers could be genuinely self-determining. They would have direct and organic access to the means of production, which would be *theirs*. Labour-power and means of production would be united once again. No sale of either labour-power or means of production would transpire.

Democracy *between* workers, rather than the tyranny of capital *over* workers, would become possible. Workers, united, would freely associate to share control of the means of production.

This requires the self-organisation of workers and their friends to advance beyond capitalism -- to produce for need rather than profit -- to create a new and truly free society.

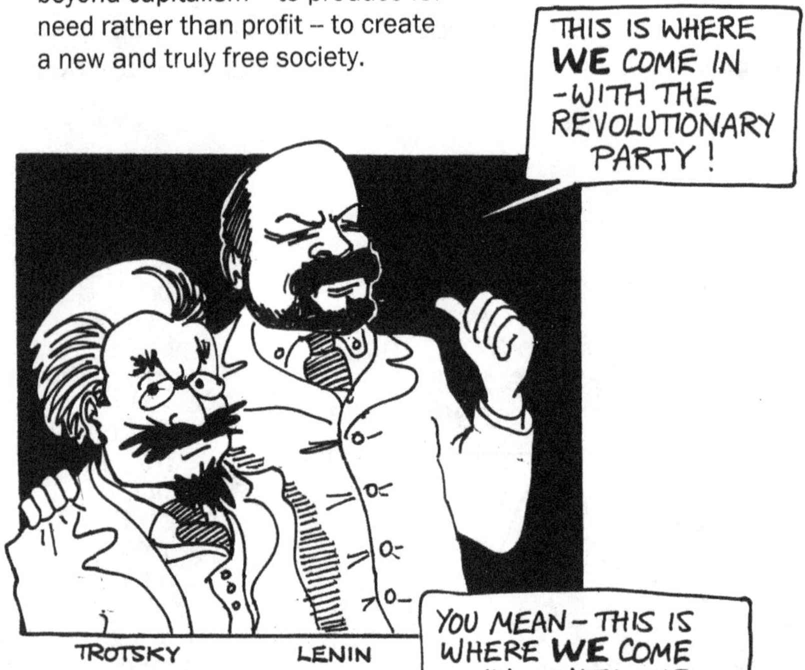
THIS IS WHERE **WE** COME IN -WITH THE REVOLUTIONARY PARTY !
TROTSKY
LENIN

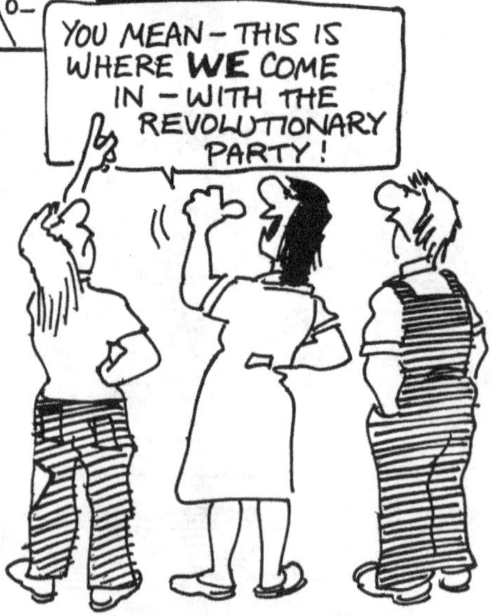
YOU MEAN - THIS IS WHERE **WE** COME IN - WITH THE REVOLUTIONARY PARTY !

Marx, unlike many later "Marxists," did not call for a "vanguard party" to rule in the name of the proletariat.

Rather, Marx wanted workers to *take matters into their own hands* – to be *self-determining*.

Lessons about the potential for reconstituting society on a radically democratic, socialist foundation can be gleaned from a renewed look at the Paris Commune, which was, for Marx, the prototype of workers' self-rule.

NAPOLEON'S STATUE, TOPPLED WITH THE
VENDOME COLUMN DURING THE PARIS COMMUNE

Though the reconstitution of society is staggeringly difficult -- the Paris Commune, don't forget, was defeated, and France, though home to a lively socialist tradition, remains a bastion of capitalism – the promise is also vast. Socialist ideas, though maligned and watered down on all sides, have percolated to every corner of the globe, and remain a vital resource. Many millions of jobless and ill-paid workers and former farmers sense that capitalism has a limited future.
That could very well be true.

Trade unions and socialist parties are necessary for working people to act in concert, whether for self-emancipation or self-defence. No ruling elite will share wealth and power willingly. So nothing could be more ruinous for socialists than apologies for elitism and dictatorship, the rule of "a new boss, same as the old boss."

Socialism, as **Rosa Luxemburg** wrote, is not some sort of Christmas gift for people who accept a dictatorship *now* in the hope of achieving freedom in the future.

STALIN

DON'T LISTEN TO HER!

ONLY THE WORKING CLASS, BY ITS SELF-ACTIVITY, CAN BRING ABOUT SOCIALISM. THAT MEANS **WORKERS CONTROL.** NOBODY CAN BRING ABOUT SOCIALISM 'ON YOUR BEHALF'...

ROSA LUXEMBURG

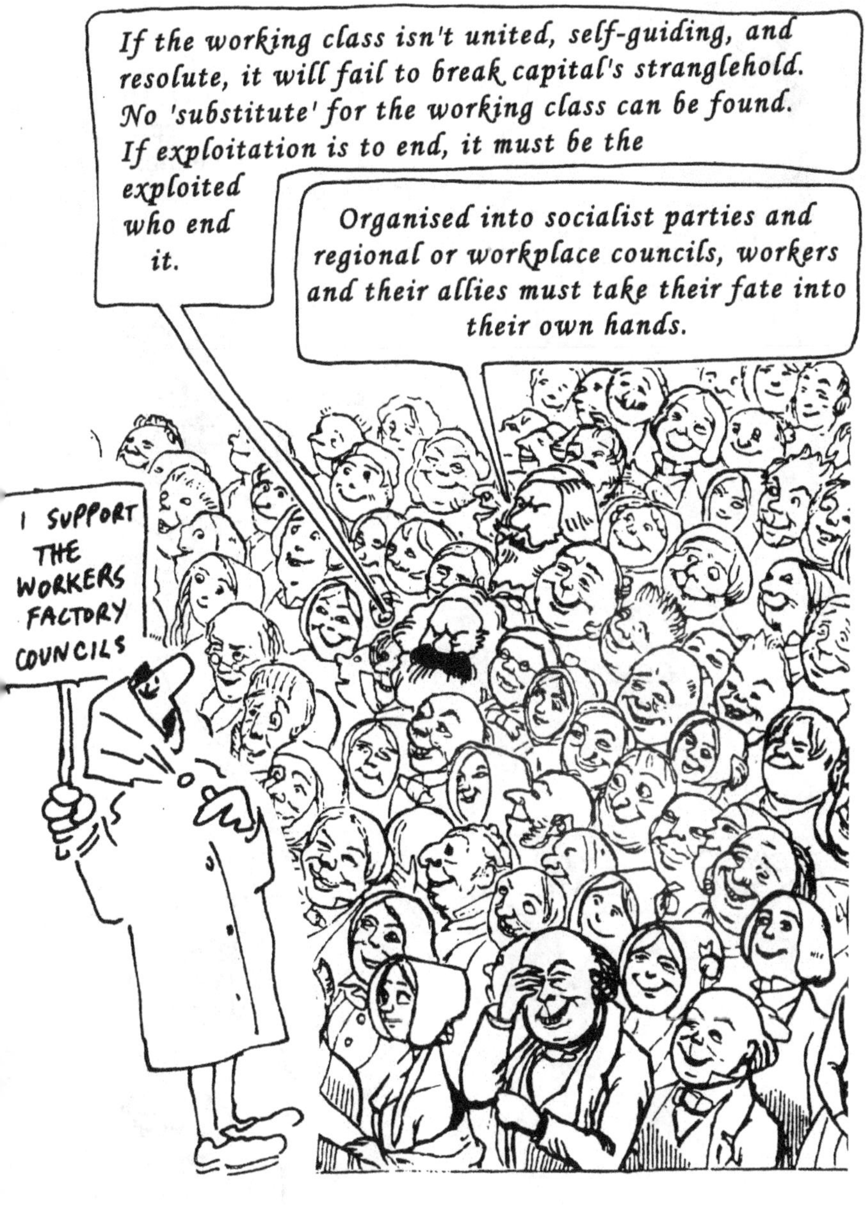
If the working class isn't united, self-guiding, and resolute, it will fail to break capital's stranglehold. No 'substitute' for the working class can be found. If exploitation is to end, it must be the exploited who end it.
Organised into socialist parties and regional or workplace councils, workers and their allies must take their fate into their own hands.
I SUPPORT THE WORKERS FACTORY COUNCILS

This is what happened in Paris, in 1871, with the formation of the Commune. Though the radical democracy and cooperation of the revolutionary Paris uprising didn't last—it was crushed by force of arms—the spirit and aims of the Communards radiated outwards to tens and hundreds of millions in the decades which followed.

Some Paris revolutionaries— **Blanqui,** for example—had elitist misconceptions about what the revolution portended. Though an admirable and indomitable agitator, Blanqui failed to see that the proletariat must organise *as a class* for revolutionary change.

BLANQUI SPENT 45 YEARS IN FRENCH PRISONS.

SINCE BLANQUI CONCEIVES OF EVERY REVOLUTION AS THE **COUP DE MAIN** OF A SMALL REVOLUTIONARY MINORITY, WHAT FOLLOWS OF ITSELF IS THE NECESSITY OF DICTATORSHIP AFTER ITS SUCCESS – THE DICTATORSHIP, PLEASE NOTE, NOT OF THE ENTIRE REVOLUTIONARY CLASS, THE PROLETARIAT, BUT OF THE SMALL NUMBER WHO MADE THE **COUP DE MAIN** AND WHO LIKEWISE ARE ORGANISED BEFOREHAND UNDER THE DICTATORSHIP OF ONE OR A FEW INDIVIDUALS.   ENGELS

I HOPE YOU'RE NOT REFERRING TO **ME**, ENGELS!

When mass movements slumber, trade unions and grassroots groups must take the initiative. But however large or small the effort, the goal, for Marx, is always the *self*-emancipation and *self*-government of the working class. Unlike many later "Marxists," Marx held that workers should not organize and sacrifice to empower dictators and elites. They should rather seek to free themselves from bosses of *all* kinds.

THE EXPROPRIATORS ARE EXPROPRIATED

'With the entanglement of all peoples in the net of the world market–and with this, the growth of the international character of the capitalist regime– there arises a world proletariat, *and a growing revolt of the proletariat. This* exploited class, prevented by capital from realising its potential for freedom and unrestrained productivity, may yet oppose itself to the capitalist integument. This integument is burst asunder. The knell of capitalist private property sounds. The expropriators are expropriated.'

and that's
not all folks!

Next comes freedom.

The Crash and After
Capitalism in Crisis?

Capitalism was sailing through rough waters when the first edition of this book appeared in 1982. The recession that year was the worst since the 1930s, and only the "Great Recession" has proved more devastating since then. What will come next? There is reason to believe that we have even harder times ahead of us.

THE FIRE THIS TIME...

Capitalism now appears to be in genuine crisis. This crisis has many unexpected features, and yet, in many ways, it resembles the crises described (and foretold) by Marx in *Das Kapital.*

Capitalism is profit-challenged and job-destroying.

It is destabilized by imbalances between profits and pay, productivity and demand, machinery and living labor.

Jobless workers and landless farmers are exiled from the workforce, as production stalls and wages fall.

Investors, fleeing production, are unable to find salvation in speculative finance.

THUS SPAKE MARX

Now, we begin to see what happens next. Investors, who increasingly invest in government bonds rather than in industry or finance, are finding this inadequate, too.

Governments have trouble paying bondholders, since they rely for revenue on workers who are increasingly wage-deprived and corporations which are increasingly tax-sheltered.

For bondholders, the solution is **"AUSTERITY"** -- service and job cuts, and tax hikes for everyone except the wealthy. A new generation of austerity politicians is pressing these policies.

INCREASINGLY, THIS PITS POLITICIANS AGAINST PUBLICS.

This conflict is likely to intensify, since hard-pressed workers and taxpayers must be squeezed ever more harshly, if the bond markets are to thrive.

Capitalism, in short, is sparking a new era of crisis-born *conflicts*. These conflicts include, but transcend, traditional class conflicts. Workers, taxpayers, the poor and needy -- all are threatened. And therein hangs a tale...

IT ALL STARTED IN THE SEVENTIES...

Competent analysts differ about whether the global economy has been "in crisis" in the past few decades. But two points seem plain: first, that capitalism is now in serious trouble, and second, that this trouble began in the 1970s and early 1980s.

The 1982 recession was a decade in the making. The most obvious causes included the failure of the gold standard in 1971 and the "oil shock" of 1973.

A happy ending? Well, not exactly.

At least, not at first...

CAPITAL VOL. I

The dollar, the world's principal currency, was no longer backed by gold, and oil prices soared.

I'm oil shocked!! Shocked, I tell you!

The global economy wobbled through a shaky decade and then stumbled into a sharp recession.

By late 1982, the US jobless rate had risen to nearly 11%.

IT SEEMED THAT *GOLD AND OIL* HAD RUN AMOK.

But deeper forces were at work. Perhaps the most decisive was an underlying profit crisis.

Profit rates have been under siege since the '70s. A top global management consulting firm calculates that, if the rate of investment in industry had held steady from 1975-2008, **20 trillion extra dollars** would have been invested in manufacturing -- money that was, instead, invested **outside manufacturing**.

A trillion here, a trillion there -- pretty soon you're talking <u>real</u> money!

WHERE DID THIS MONEY GO?

Nearly everywhere -- *except industry.*

Investors became increasingly reluctant to invest in manufacturing. After a century of concentrated industrial investment, they opted for "high-yield" alternatives outside production. Many such investments were **SPECULATIVE***.*

THIS WAS OFTEN CALLED WILD WEST CAPITALISM, OR "VENTURE CAPITALISM"*...*

"Speculation, where the rich get richer by the day!*

"Where money makes money, and stock markets soar.

"Where debt's a bet, and gambles always pay...."

**Sung to the tune of "Oklahoma." Apologies to Oscar Hammerstein!*

WE JUNK BONDS...

High-risk "junk" bonds attracted hordes of investment banks in the 1980s, led by Drexel Burnham Lambert. Leading industrial firms like Chrysler and International Harvester had fallen on hard times, and junk bonds, in contrast, seemed immune to downturns.

Gambling on junk bonds, Drexel Burnham soon rivalled even Goldman Sachs for supremacy among investment banks ....before collapsing in 1990.

WE  DOT COMS...

Investors gambled on the internet in the late '90s. Instead of investing in established firms, they poured money into the new '**DOT.COMS**,' which offered free internet services in the hope that, ultimately, they could *sell* these services for a *profit*.

Investors thought that companies that attract so much money...must be fabulously valuable. They were mistaken. Dizzying sums went to dot.coms that yielded <u>**no profit at all**</u>. In 2000, the main Stock Exchange for high tech stocks rose to a peak, fueled by dreamy optimism -- and then it crashed. Dot.coms lost trillions. Most went bankrupt.

WE DERIVATIVES...

Undaunted, investors pursued financial schemes into the 21st century. Vast sums extracted from industry went into speculation, where they were used to buy risky mortgage debt ("securitized," insured, and resold) and "derivatives" (which, often, were contracts to buy future debt).

183

In 2008 this house of cards crashed. *The epic crisis that ensued, the "Great Recession," has not been followed by a Great Recovery...*

Globally, hundreds of millions of workers remain out of work, and consumer demand remains perilously weak...

CAPITALISM IN QUESTION

It now seems possible that capitalism could fall apart altogether -- a disconcerting prospect that comfortable pundits once dismissed as soft-headed doom-saying.

Today, even organs of the business press like the *Financial Times* and *Wall Street Journal* routinely admit the danger.

Why? Because speculation has proven dangerous. Each of the financial bubbles that led to recent recessions (in 1990-1991, 2000-2001, and 2007-2010) was followed by a long, severe, and "jobless" recovery. *And yet, speculation has not abated.*

European investment in junk bonds peaked...in 2010.

What Alan Greenspan, who then chaired the Federal Reserve Board, famously called "irrational exuberance" in 1996 has sprung back to life.

Stock markets soar, and doubters are doubted...

"This time will be different," investors think. "This time, speculation *won't* end in disaster."

But speculation is always potentially disastrous -- not just as a form of gambling, but as a diversion *from productive investment.* **Money spent on speculative finance is money withheld from production**. Without production, jobs and wages fall and demand plunges.

IS THIS EVEN STILL CAPITALISM?

Today, it often seems that the defining aim of investment is no longer the classical capitalist goal of *profiting from the production and sale of commodities.*

In Marxian terms, money appears to be functioning less and less as **capital.** Rather than employing **workers** to make and sell **commodities,** money owners increasingly try to *clone* their money by purely financial means.

Is this even still capitalism? Many people wonder.
The answer may be that capitalism is now in <u>twilight</u>.
Industry is still essential and profit is still the name of the
game. But today few institutional members of the global
investing class (investment banks, asset management firms,
hedge funds, sovereign wealth funds, bond buyers, etc.)
even consider investing in new production. Just about
any starry-eyed scheme draws a crowd of
investors -- but industry? *Seldom.*

Even *corporations* now tend to abstain from production.

We're people too,
you know!
(When we prick you,
do you not bleed?)

GE Capital

Many industrial firms "diversify" into finance,
so that General Motors and General Electric,
for example (both of which remain
industrial icons), now derive much
of their revenue from finance.

And corporations, in general,
increasingly withhold
investment from
industry.

But we still hire service workers!

187

Currently, thanks to tax breaks and government "stimulus" measures, US corporations have more money than ever before -- and yet they hoard much of their money, reluctant to produce for the soft consumer market.

When they do invest in production, they seem to invest with an eye-dropper.

Factories are SO 20th century!

JOB KILLERS

Capitalists are praised, in the rhetoric of politics, as "job creators." And yet factory jobs are increasingly relegated to "rust belts" in the advanced economies and coastal slivers of "less developed countries." Jobs that survive the onslaught of corporate cutbacks are normally speeded up or "offshored" to low-wage havens.

It is emblematic of 21st-century capitalism that the paragon of commodity production today is an ultra-low wage nation (China) that, until recently, claimed to be...non-capitalist!

"If it walks like a duck and quacks like a duck, it probably is a duck. Er, capitalist. (You can go back to reading the Grundrisse now.)"
John D. Duckefeller

And even China, despite its "roaring economy," re-invests only a fraction of its industrial profits. Afraid to overtax the world's consumer markets, and fearful of overheating its own economy (and driving up wages), the authoritarian regime in Beijing diverts literally trillions of dollars away from industry -- investing, above all, in foreign bonds.

The consequence is that China has more frustrated job-seekers -- more unemployed workers and landless farmers -- than any nation on earth. Former farmers, who, over several generations, were displaced from the land by the regime or by regime-connected developers, now float in a paupers' broth of scarcity and desperation.

Only a small portion of the millions who migrate to cities find employment.

> *The factories along the Chinese coast are just a fraction, just a token, of what could exist if the regime reinvested its industrial profits unstintingly. But here as elsewhere, the profit potential of manufacturing is apparently not attractive enough to spur unfettered reinvestment in industry.*

Will China remain the world's motor? That remains to be seen. Many pundits have called this "the Chinese century." But Chinese growth in the first decade of this century was the product of an already fading reality -- a moment when Western investors and consumers were willing to borrow prodigiously and Chinese workers were willing to work for nearly nothing.

That unique combination of circumstances seems unlikely to return. Western consumers are in retreat and Chinese workers are restive. Global industry, from Beijing to Berlin, has few obvious long-term prospects.

> Capitalism stands at the brink of a kind of entropy. The capital "flight" of the recent past is giving way to capital *paralysis*. Immense sums of money, with few profitable outlets, are immobile, barred to jobless workers and revenue-starved states. Money now risks becoming *useless*...

I call this "the Law of Marginal Futility"!

CALLING DR. MARX

All of this connects, in the most basic way, to Marx's theory in *Capital*. According to Marx, capitalism has a chronic, intrinsic profit problem.

(Psst.... *See Chapter 16*. Or at least read the *Grundrisse*.)

Even as the **MASS OF PROFIT** soars, often to stratospheric heights, the **PROFIT RATE**, per dollar of investment, tends to fall.

*Why? Because profit, like all surplus value, derives from the surplus labor of **WORKERS**, not (as many people suppose) from investment in **TECHNOLOGY**.*

Workers, not machines, are the fount of profit. The total **mass** of profit increases with productivity, which machines *facilitate.* But, for profit **rates** to stay intact, investment in "variable capital" *(living human labor power)* must match or exceed investment in "constant capital" *(machines and other means of production).*

...ively, but not lively enough.
...'m automating!

THAT RARELY HAPPENS. Rather, investment in constant capital tends to outstrip investment in variable capital.

RECENT HISTORY SHOWS THIS CLEARLY.

Since the Depression of the 1930s, the ratio of constant to variable capital (investment in **c** relative to **v**) has steadily and strikingly increased.

THE COUNTRY CANNOT AFFORD EXORBITANT WAGE DEMANDS...

Episodes of good luck (market opportunities, etc.) have occasionally allowed profit surges. And capitalists have enjoyed vast wealth, even as their rate of profit per product has declined.

ALL MAJOR CREDIT CARDS ACCEPTED

But in the longer run, as the composition of capital changes -- as **c** rises relative to **v** -- profit rates fall steadily and the viability of investment in production becomes doubtful.

It's like global warming. An occasional freezing winter doesn't mean that warming isn't the **main** trend.

WAGES

A little warming would be okay!

That's because, as we saw earlier...

WE HAVE **CRISES**...WHEN **C RISES**

Clearly, *c* has been **rising**. Does that explain our **crisis**?

My answer is: ***PROBABLY, PARTLY.***

PROBABLY -- It seems quite possible that the rate of profit has been falling for decades. Otherwise, when speculation falters, the rate of investment in production should revive. But that tends to happen rarely, and briefly -- if at all.

That's why we call these recoveries "jobless"!

Can we say definitively that profit rates have fallen?

No, since the key facts (world-wide price, production, and profit data, gathered reliably over time) are available only in part. But the available evidence **does** clearly show that in key sectors of the global economy (for example, in the United States) industrial profit rates have fallen steadily in recent years, while speculation has spiraled upward.

PARTLY -- Another tendency is also now relevant, which we can call the rising *financial* composition of capitalism. As the profitability of investment in **c** and **v** falls, money owners are tempted to invest in finance instead. Money, siphoned from **c** and **v** into finance, *ceases to be productive capital.*

At first glance, speculative and productive profits might seem interchangeable. But since no new value arises in finance, money that transfers from production to finance vanishes from value-creation.

Financial profits may look good on paper, when speculative bubbles inflate; but these "profits" are often little more than numbers in a computer. Capital, as such, does not accumulate.

WHAT GOES UP,
MUST COME DOWN

Speculative bubbles inflate...and pop. So speculation can compensate for falling profit rates only temporarily. Better, for investors who have not forsaken production, is to increase surplus value in standard ways: *relatively,* by producing faster or more efficiently, or *absolutely,* by extending the working day or by substituting lower paid labor for higher paid labor, either at home or abroad.

All such measures are "counter-tendencies" to the falling profit rate. All have been effective, to varying degrees, in the immediate past.

The cure for falling profits? Falling wages!

Cutting wages is easier when the demand for labor falls; and relocating production to low-wage destinations (the "maquiladora" zone in northern Mexico, southern coastal China) is easier when transportation improves -- as happened, for example, in the 1970s, with the emergence of containerized freight.

These measures often *work.* They can slow or reverse falling profit rates. But even so, manufacturing today remains sluggish. The usual ways of buoying profits seem to be losing their punch.

In the unsettled wake of the Great Recession -- with Europe in peril, Chinese industry slowing down, and financial gambling on the rise -- the future of capitalism is uncertain at best.

CAN WE GET THERE FROM HERE?

Many investors, in the new climate, are shedding their skins. Rather than profiting from the exploitation of workers *in production,* they seek profit from the *taxation* of workers -- *outside* of production. They invest in government bonds, hoping for rich returns from tax hikes and spending cuts.

Don't you dare call this "taxploitation"!

But this isn't working very well. The problem is that governments are facing a new kind of fiscal crisis. Here are the lineaments of that crisis:

1. *State revenues are in disarray.* Globalized businesses pay fewer and fewer taxes, and workers are less and less *capable* of paying taxes. This puts governments at the mercy of bond investors, whose lending becomes a partial substitute for tax revenue. *Increasingly,*

> ## Capitalists **won't** pay taxes...
> ## and workers **can't** pay taxes.

2. *Bond markets "come to the rescue."* Investors, burned by speculative failures and reluctant to return to industry, have increasingly turned to government bonds, as a "safe harbor" from the vicissitudes of financial and commercial markets.

3. This sounds win-win. Governments need revenue and investors need investment outlets. Both needs are satisfied when investors buy government bonds. *But in reality both governments and investors face a kind of Catch-22 in this situation -- a grave crisis, with grave consequences.*

4. The dilemma is that governments have trouble paying bondholders for the very same reason that they sold them bonds in the first place -- because their tax base has eroded. They sell bonds today and must sell more tomorrow *because taxes are not sufficient to keep governments operational.* But their ability to repay the bondholders is hobbled by their tax deficit.

THE CONSEQUENCE? Bondholders demand pay, and governments are pressured to comply. Politicians become accomplices to bondholders --

who demand strict austerity, even during a recession.

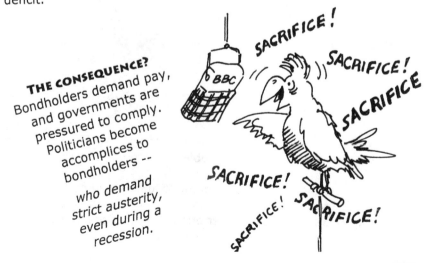

THE PAIN IS IMMEDIATE.
Public workers lose their jobs and
the needy are deprived of assistance. But even
austerity politicians can't get blood from stones. Workers
can't pay in taxes what they don't get in wages. Like just
about everyone else (the jobless, landless, and helpless)
they are in *need* of money, not sources of money.

Hungry?
Just tighten
your belt!

Money-owners, meanwhile, hesitate to spend their money,
because they can't find reliable ways to become richer.

The morbid result is a world divided between cash-rich
investors, who hesitate to invest, and cash-poor wage
workers, who have fewer and fewer chances to work
for wages.

It's all downhill from here, Fred!

THE WHEELS OF COMMERCE COULD SLOW AND STOP. WILL THEY?

In the short run, recovery is possible.

Speculators, ever inventive, are inflating new bubbles. Central banks are pouring new money into the economy on a monumental scale -- *spending over 2 trillion dollars in the U.S. alone in just over 2 years* -- mainly to buy bonds from commercial banks. This artificially boosted the bond market, lifted stock prices to soaring heights, and vastly enriched investors.

China has pledged to shift from export-oriented production to manufacturing and service for the domestic consumer market.

That could help revive Western industry, for a while.
Government defaults could be averted, for a while.

But longer-term recovery is unlikely
unless the towering mass of
immobilized capital is
destroyed on a
grand scale.

Otherwise,
profit rates and
industrial investment
are likely to remain stagnant.

Historically, the destruction of useless capital has permitted
capitalism to revive after previous crises. But burning off
excess capital would cause bankruptcies and job loss. It
seems likely, given the uprecedented global scale and
impact of such a crisis today, that the outcome of
bankruptcies and mass job loss would be
system failure rather than recovery.

In the meantime (*and it is, indeed, a very mean time*), zealous bondholders and their political accomplices are forcing budget cuts and tax hikes so severe that publics everywhere --

workers and ex-workers, farmers and ex-farmers, taxpayers and former taxpayers -- increasingly

share an interest in anti-austerity resistance.

INSURRECTION ON A SLAVE SHIP

Will solidarity be the outcome? Will people refuse to let money (absent on side, overabundant on the other) rule their fates?

Can we even imagine a world without money as its oxygen, its pivot, its center of gravity?

A world where people cooperate rather than competing, where we share rather than selling?

That unlikely world, it now seems, may be precisely what we need to survive in an age when money is barred to the vast majority. If states default and workers lose their jobs -- if wages fall, markets falter, and capital is frozen -- will people still treat money as the sole valid motive for work and production?

Will the exploited and expropriated reject cooperation? Will they work shoulder to shoulder only under the sign of capital, only in return for a paycheck, even in the worst of crises? Will we accept global joblessness and global warming rather than put need ahead of profit?

Marx was hopeful that, staring into the abyss, the exploited and expropriated would join forces to emancipate and save themselves, abolishing class rule and building a society of freely associated producers.

This might have been naive -- but our generation, and the next one, may have the chance to vindicate that hope. If Marx was right, our very survival hangs in the balance.

Read more!

Tempted as we might be to settle for secondary sources -- like this one -- there really is no substitute for the original. *Capital* is the only work that even attempts to explain the capitalist system as a whole, and Marx's brilliance shines through thousands of pages of subtle analysis.

Marx's best critics concede his strengths even as they disagree with him. Böhm-Bawerk, "the lion of the anti-Marxists," once said that, if we accept Marx's premises, everything else follows with iron necessity; but alas, he added, Marx's premises are fatally flawed.

Marx's readers should accept Böhm-Bawerk's challenge. They should bend every effort to grasp Marx's premises, to judge for themselves whether his argument goes astray at the start – or, rather, makes sense of a senseless system.

UNDER SOCIALISM
THEY'D MAKE US
ALL THE SAME...

Marx's most basic premise is the notion of the commodity. We live, he says, in a *Warenwelt* -- a world of commodities. Although Marx is usually credited with a "theory of value," he wrote, late in life, that his outlook is better characterized as *a theory of the commodity.*

This could seem to be a trivial distinction, since the commodity, for Marx, is the contradictory unity of use-value *and value.* But in reality this distinction is vital.

Value, as portrayed by Marx, is an *obstacle* to use -- a kind of social force field around labor products that blocks our access to them.

Only money can pierce this field and give people access to what they need; and money, too, is a commodity.

Money, indeed, is the commodity "universally equivalent" to all others. As such, it is the *ultimate* commodity. Without it, we can have nothing *else.*

MONEY IS THE ROOT OF ALL EXCHANGE!

(GOLD, ANYONE? I'LL TRADE A GOLD BAR FOR A CANDY BAR!)

Money is thus a *survival obstacle* for anyone without it. But that's only true because we *allow* value to block use.

In capitalist society, products aren't used until after they sell -- *if* they sell. So, if we lack money, we are denied everything – however abundant.

TOO MANY HOMES BEING BUILT
- LATEST WIGAN WORKERS COUNCIL REPORT

(Or rare! In 2011, a first edition of *Das Kapital,* dedicated by Marx to his friend E.S. Beesly, was put up for sale...for over $500,000!)

Keenly aware of the limits placed by the profit motive on the satisfaction of human need, Marx advocated a *money-free, commodity-free, value-free society* - a society, in short, in which people simply *share* what they make and share *decision-making power*, without bosses or profits.

IS THIS EVEN POSSIBLE?

According to Marx -- *yes, absolutely* – and ultimately, it is commodity production and the money system, not cooperation and sharing, that are unsustainable. To understand why Marx believed this, we need to know what he meant by the words **commodity, money, and value**.

That requires attention, above all, to the opening chapter of *Capital* Vol. 1, "The Commodity."

This chapter is best known in the version that appeared in the third German edition, translated well by Ben Fowkes (1976). But Albert Dragstedt's translation of the first edition of *Capital 1,* Chapter 1, is also essential, since Marx explains several points there with unmatched clarity:

WWW.MARXISTS.ORG/ARCHIV E/MARX/WORKS/ 1867– C1/COMMODITY.HTM

Marx's early work, *Zur Kritik der politischen Ökonomie* (known in English as *A Contribution to the Critique of Political Economy*, 1859) also merits careful attention.

Some of the themes in the first chapter add nuance to the argument in the first chapter of *Capital 1*, and the ensuing chapter – on money – is the single most detailed account of money in any of Marx's works.

www.marxists.org/archive/marx/works/1859/critique-pol-economy/

Adolf Wagner
Marx's critic and foil

Marx's 1879 reading notes on a book by the economist Adolf Wagner are also important. Here Marx explained what he meant when he said that *Capital* offers a theory of the commodity, not simply a theory of value.

www.marxists.org/archive/marx/works/1881/01/wagner.htm

Serious readers, of course, will want to study the rest of *Capital as well*. That includes not only Vols. 2 and 3 (of which "Vol. 2" is Marx's essential final text; "Vol. 3" was written before Vol. 1), but also, appended to the Viking edition of Vol. 1, the fundamental but overlooked manuscript "Results of the Immediate Production Process."

ALSO WORTH READING

ON CAPITAL
ROSA LUXEMBURG, *THE ACCUMULATION OF CAPITAL* (LONDON: ROUTLEDGE, 2003). ROMAN ROSDOLSKY, *THE MAKING OF MARX'S 'CAPITAL'*, VOLS. 1 & 2 (LONDON: PLUTO, 1992). DIANE ELSON, *VALUE* (LONDON: CSE BOOKS AND HUMANITIES, 1979).

ON CAPITALISM TODAY
CHRIS HARMAN, *ZOMBIE CAPITALISM: GLOBAL CRISIS AND THE RELEVANCE OF MARX* (CHICAGO: HAYMARKET, 2010). ANDREW KLIMAN, *THE FAILURE OF CAPITALIST PRODUCTION* (LONDON: PLUTO, 2011, ESPECIALLY CHAPTER 5 ON THE PROFIT RATE).

ON MARX'S POLITICS
HAL DRAPER, *KARL MARX'S THEORY OF REVOLUTION*, VOLS. 1-5 (NEW YORK: MONTHLY REVIEW, 1977-2010). RAYA DUNAYEVSKAYA, *MARXISM AND FREEDOM* (AMHERST, NY: HUMANITY, 2000). PETER HUDIS, *MARX'S CONCEPT OF THE ALTERNATIVE TO CAPITALISM* (CHICAGO: HAYMARKET, 2013).

ON MARX'S WORLDVIEW
RICHARD LICHTMAN, *THE PRODUCTION OF DESIRE: THE INTEGRATION OF PSYCHOANALYSIS INTO MARXIST THEORY* (NEW YORK: FREE PRESS, 1982). KEVIN ANDERSON, *MARX AT THE MARGINS: ON NATIONALISM, ETHNICITY, AND NON-WESTERN SOCIETIES* (CHICAGO: UNIVERSITY OF CHICAGO, 2010).

ON CAPITAL AND CULTURE
MICHAEL TAUSSIG, *THE DEVIL AND COMMODITY FETISHISM IN SOUTH AMERICA* (CHAPEL HILL: THE UNIVERSITY OF NORTH CAROLINA, 2010). DEAN WOLFE MANDERS, *THE HEGEMONY OF COMMON SENSE* (NEW YORK: PETER LANG, 2006).

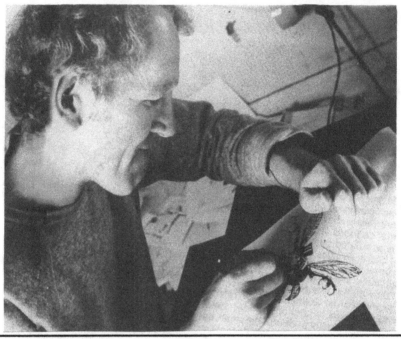

Cartoonist Phil Evans (1946-2014), at work on the art for page 33.

Photo by Jackie Lecanu

Phil Evans was a veteran humorist and activist whose art graced many books, including, besides this volume, *Trotsky for Beginners* by Tariq Ali; *London for Beginners* by Nita Clarke; *Understanding Economics* by Ken Cole; *Why You Should Be A Socialist* by Paul Foot; and *More Years for the Locust* by Jim Higgins. Evans was the author and illustrator of *Ireland for Beginners*, with Eileen Pollock.

Before he turned to books, Evans penned a popular comic strip, "Our Norman," for the socialist press in Britain, and he provided art for countless pamphlets, flyers, and more. Readers can enjoy his early work in *The Joke Works: The Political Cartoons of Phil Evans*, edited by Steve Irons and prefaced by Dave Widgery.

Appreciations of Phil Evans' cartoon artistry by Kent Worcester are available online. See, for example, *http://classic.tcj.com/alternative/phil-evans-once-more-with-feeling/*

About Haymarket Books

Haymarket Books is a nonprofit, progressive book distributor and publisher, a project of the Center for Economic Research and Social Change. We believe that activists need to take ideas, history, and politics into the many struggles for social justice today. Learning the lessons of past victories, as well as defeats, can arm a new generation of fighters for a better world. As Karl Marx said, "The philosophers have merely interpreted the world; the point, however, is to change it."

We take inspiration and courage from our namesakes, the Haymarket Martyrs, who gave their lives fighting for a better world. Their 1886 struggle for the eight-hour day, which gave us May Day, the international workers' holiday, reminds workers around the world that ordinary people can organize and struggle for their own liberation. These struggles continue today across the globe—struggles against oppression, exploitation, hunger, and poverty.

It was August Spies, one of the Martyrs targeted for being an immigrant and an anarchist, who predicted the battles being fought to this day. "If you think that by hanging us you can stamp out the labor movement," Spies told the judge, "then hang us. Here you will tread upon a spark, but here, and there, and behind you, and in front of you, and everywhere, the flames will blaze up. It is a subterranean fire. You cannot put it out. The ground is on fire upon which you stand."

We could not succeed in our publishing efforts without the generous financial support of our readers. Many people contribute to our project through the Haymarket Book Club, where donors receive every title Haymarket Books publishes for just $30 per month. If you would like to join the book club, please visit our website or contact us at info@haymarketbooks.org.

Shop our full catalog online at www.haymarketbooks.org or call 773-583-7884.

Also from Haymarket Books

The Meaning of Marxism
Paul D'Amato
Long-considered dead by mainstream critics, the basic ideas of Karl Marx are brought to life in this overview of his thought. This book argues that instead of irrelevant, Marx's ideas of globalization, oppression, and social change are more important than ever.

The Communist Manifesto
A Road Map to History's Most Important Political Document
Phil Gasper (Editor), Karl Marx, Fredrick Engels
Here, at last, is an authoritative introduction to history's most important political document, with the full text of The Communist Manifesto by Marx and Engels.

This beautifully organized and presented edition of The Communist Manifesto is fully annotated, with clear historical references and explication, additional related texts, and a glossary that will bring the text to life for students, as well as the general reader.

Since it was first written in 1848, the Manifesto has been translated into more languages than any other modern text. It has been banned, censored, burned, and declared "dead." But year after year, the text only grows more influential, remaining required reading in courses on philosophy, politics, economics, and history.

The Revolutionary Ideas of Karl Marx
Alex Callinicos
In this engaging and accessible introduction, Alex Callinicos demonstrates that Marx's ideas hold an enduring relevance for today's activists fighting against poverty, inequality, oppression, environmental destruction, and the numerous other injustices of the capitalist system.

Leon Trotsky
An Illustrated Introduction
Tariq Ali and Phil Evans
Amusing, well researched, and surprisingly sophisticated, *Leon Trotsky: An Illustrated Introduction* is the perfect primer on the life and thought of the great leader and chronicler of the Russian Revolution. With sympathy and humor, Tariq Ali and Phil Evans trace his political career, from prison to the pinnacle of revolutionary power to his eventual exile and murder by Joseph Stalin.